CW01670178

LIFE IN CHRIST

POPE FRANCIS
ON BAPTISM, CONFIRMATION AND THE TEN COMMANDMENTS

Preface by Monsignor Guido Marini

All books are published thanks to the generosity of the supporters of the Catholic Truth Society

CATHOLIC TRUTH SOCIETY

Life in Christ, *first published 2020 by The Incorporated Catholic Truth Society, 42-46 Harleyford Road London SE11 5AY Tel: 020 7640 0042 Fax: 020 7640 0046 Website: www.ctsbooks.org.*

CTS Code: DO953 ISBN: 978 1 78469 643 6

Printed in Great Britain by Bell and Bain Ltd, Glasgow

Contents

THE SACRAMENTS

Baptism

Confirmation

THE TEN COMMANDMENTS

PREFACE

It is often true that we can more easily discover the heart of a long journey by carefully considering its last stage. This is the case with the series of catecheses that the Holy Father, Pope Francis, gave during his Wednesday general audiences, presenting and exploring first the subject of the Sacraments and then that of the Commandments.

This is why it is very helpful to pay close attention to the last catechesis the Pope dedicated to the Decalogue. This catechesis sets the great law of Sinai in the light of the full revelation of Christ. "But to live in this way - that is, in the beauty of fidelity, generosity and authenticity - we need a new heart, inhabited by the Holy Spirit (cf. *Ez* 11:19; 36:26). I wonder: how does this "heart transplant", from an old heart to a new heart, come about? It happens through the gift of new desires (cf. *Rom* 8:6) that are sown in us by the grace of God, in a particular way, through the Ten Commandments fulfilled by Jesus, as he teaches in the Sermon on the Mount (cf. *Mt* 5:15-48). Indeed, in contemplating the life described in the Decalogue - that is, a grateful, free, authentic, blessed, adult existence, as guardian and lover of a steadfast, generous and sincere life - we stand before Christ again, almost without realising it. The Decalogue is his 'x-ray': it is like a photographic negative that lets his face appear - as it does in the Holy Shroud. And thus the Holy Spirit renders our heart fruitful, placing in it desires that are his gift, the desires of the Spirit: to desire according to the Spirit, to desire with the rhythm of the Spirit, to desire with the music of the Spirit. Looking to Christ we see beauty, goodness, truth. And the Spirit engenders a life that, supporting these desires of his, kindles hope, faith and love in us."

God's plan entails the heart transplant that brings to our life the gift of a new heart. Ultimately it is precisely here that the joy of the Gospel is rooted: the proclamation of this extraordinary grace, the fulfilment of an ancient promise, unthinkable and expected at the same time, through which it becomes possible to live the very life of God in Christ. "In Christ, and in him alone, the Decalogue ceases to be a condemnation (cf. *Rom* 8:1) and becomes the authentic truth of human life, namely, a desire for love - a desire for good, to do good is born here - a desire for joy, for peace, for magnanimity, for benevolence, for goodness, for fidelity, for meekness, for self-control. It goes from that 'no' to this 'yes': the positive attitude of a heart that opens with the power of the Holy Spirit."

"It is no longer I who live, but Christ lives in me" (*Gal* 2:20). What the Apostle Paul says about himself is the common destination of every disciple of the Lord, who receives the transplant of a new heart through the gift of new desires sown by God's grace.

This, then, is the beauty of the Sacraments and of the liturgical life, a beauty that allows us to experience their transformative power. The Sacraments, in fact, are the ordinary means through which the heart transplant is realised and the new heart receives its lifeblood and nourishment. There, in the Sacraments, the risen Lord is present and active, bringing to life for us the mystery of the new covenant founded on the gift of the new heart. The Sacraments are the "today" of Christ, physician of souls and bodies, the "now" of salvation through which he comes to dwell among us, loving us to the very end.

Beginning his cycle of catecheses on the Sacraments, Pope Francis affirms: "It is really important to return to the basics, to rediscover what is essential, through what we touch and see in the celebration of the Sacraments. Remember the question of the Apostle St Thomas (cf. *Jn* 20:25), seeking to see and touch the nail wounds in Jesus's body, and his desire to be able in some way to 'touch' God in order to believe in him. What St Thomas asks of the Lord is what we all need: to see him, to touch him so that we may be able to know him. The Sacraments meet this human need. The Sacraments, and the eucharistic celebration in a particular way, are signs of God's love, the privileged ways for us to encounter him."

And in relation to the Eucharist he recalls the ever-relevant experience of the martyrs of Abitinae: "We cannot forget the great number of Christians who, throughout the world, in two thousand years of history, have died defending the Eucharist; and how many, even today, risk their lives in order to participate in Sunday Mass. In the year 304, during the Diocletianic persecution, a group of Christians from North Africa were surprised as they were celebrating Mass in a house, and were arrested. In the interrogation, the Roman Proconsul asked them why they had done this even though they knew it was absolutely prohibited. They responded: 'Without Sunday we cannot live', which meant: if we cannot celebrate the Eucharist, we cannot live; our Christian life would die."

Christian life would die. Here is the vital importance of the Sacraments and, in particular, of the Eucharist. Once again we are reminded that life in Christ is a new life, a life that is a gift, a life of grace. And this is the essence of the proclamation of joy that pervades every season of history. The beautiful, good, and true life, which is holiness, is not the result of a human achievement. Our own poor powers or our uncertain will cannot bring us to the goal of a life in keeping with God's plan. Jesus did not come in order to burden our journey by imposing other duties; he did not come to tell us, "You must do such and such." He came, instead, to free us from the unbearable weight of our misery, our inadequacy, our guilt, our inevitable death. He came to give us true freedom, to proclaim that, by virtue of the salvation that he has wrought, it is possible to live the life of God, a wondrous new life lived in beauty, in goodness, in truth. The words that resound from the lips of the Risen One are "You can!"; and this becomes, for all those who welcome it, the door of entry to that life in Christ which is also the only truly human life.

In truth, the Commandments point to a way of life which, in faint outline, reveals the face of Christ; by the power of the Sacraments, this becomes a path we can travel, leading all the way to the heights of the life of holiness. It is then indeed that "In Christ, and in him alone, the Decalogue ceases to be a condemnation (cf. *Rom* 8:1) and becomes the authentic truth of human life."

Mgr. Guido Marini
Master of Pontifical Liturgical Celebrations

The Sacraments

BAPTISM

The Foundation of Christian Life

The Sign of the Christian Faith

The Strength to Overcome Evil

Source of Life

Regeneration

Clothed with Christ

The Foundation of Christian Life

The fifty days of liturgical Easter Time are propitious for reflecting on Christian life, which, by its nature, is the life which comes from Christ himself. We are, in fact, Christians to the extent that we allow Jesus Christ to live in us. Where, then, do we begin to rekindle this awareness, if not from the beginning, from the *Sacrament which ignited Christian life within us*?

This is *Baptism*. Christ's Passover, charged with newness, reaches us through Baptism in order to transform us into his image: the baptised *belong to Jesus Christ*. He is the *Lord* of their existence. "Baptism is the basis of the whole Christian life" (*Catechism of the Catholic Church*, n. 1213). It is the first of the Sacraments, inasmuch as it is *the door* which allows Christ the Lord to dwell in our person and allows us to be immersed in his mystery.

The Greek word "to baptise" means "*to immerse*" (cf. CCC, n. 1214). To bathe with water is a rite common to various beliefs to express the passage from one condition to another, a sign of purification for a new beginning. But for us Christians, it must be noted that if the body is immersed in water, *the soul is immersed in Christ* in order to receive the forgiveness of sin and to shine with divine light (cf. Tertullian, *On the resurrection of the dead*, viii, 3: ccl 2, 931; pl 2, 806). By virtue of the Holy Spirit, Baptism *immerses us in the death and Resurrection of the Lord*, drowning in the baptismal font the "old" man, dominated by sin which separates him from God, and giving birth to the new man, recreated in Jesus. In him all the children of Adam are called to new life.

Therefore, Baptism is a rebirth. I am certain, quite sure, that we all remember our date of birth: certain. But I ask myself, a little doubtfully, and I ask you: do each of you recall the date of your Baptism? Some say "yes" – okay. But it is a rather weak "yes", because perhaps many do not remember this date. But if we celebrate birthdays, why not celebrate – or at least remember – the day of rebirth? I will give you a homework assignment, a task to do today at home. Those of you who do not remember the date of your Baptism, ask your mother, aunts and uncles, nieces and nephews, ask them: "Do you know the date of my Baptism?"; and never forget it. And thank the Lord for that day, because it is the very day on which Jesus entered me, the Holy Spirit entered me. Do you understand what your homework is? We should all know the date of our Baptism. It is another birthday: the date of rebirth. Do not forget to do this, please.

Let us recall the last words of the Risen One to the Apostles; they are a precise mandate: "Go therefore and make disciples of all nations, baptising them in the name of the Father and of the Son and of the Holy Spirit" (*Mt* 28:19). Through the baptismal bath, those who believe in Christ are immersed in the very life of the Trinity.

Indeed, the water of Baptism is not just any water, but the water upon which *the Spirit*, the "giver of life" (Creed) is invoked. Let us consider what Jesus said to Nicodemus in order to explain to him birth into divine life: "unless one is born of water and the Spirit, he cannot enter the kingdom of God. That which is born of the flesh is flesh, and that which is born of the Spirit is spirit" (*Jn* 3:5-6). Thus Baptism is also called "*regeneration*": we believe that God has saved us "in virtue of his own mercy, by the washing of regeneration and renewal in the Holy Spirit" (*Tit* 3:5).

Baptism is therefore an effective sign of rebirth, in order to walk in the newness of life. St Paul reminds the Christians of Rome about this: "Do you not know that all of us who have been baptised into Christ Jesus were baptised into his death? We were buried therefore with him by baptism into death, so that as Christ was raised from the dead by the glory of the Father, we too might walk in newness of life" (*Rom* 6:3-4).

By immersing us in Christ, Baptism also makes us *members of his Body, which is the Church*, and sharers in her mission in the world (cf. CCC, n. 1213). We baptised are not isolated: we are members of the Body of Christ. The vitality which springs forth from the baptismal font is illustrated by these words of Jesus: "I am the vine, you are the branches. He who abides in me, and I in him, he it is that bears much fruit" (*Jn* 15:5). A self-same life, that of the Holy Spirit, flows from Christ to the baptised, uniting them in one Body (cf. *1 Cor* 12:13), anointed by the holy unction and nourished at the eucharistic table.

Baptism allows Christ to live in us and allows us to live united with him, to co-operate in the Church, each according to his or her condition, for the transformation of the world. Received only once, the baptismal bath illuminates our whole life, guiding our steps all the way to the Heavenly Jerusalem. There is a before and an after to Baptism. The Sacrament presumes a journey of faith, which we call *catechumenate*, evident when it is an adult requesting Baptism. But from antiquity, children, too, have been baptised in the faith of their parents (cf. *Rite of Baptism for children*, Introduction, 2). And I would like to tell you something about this. Some people think: "But why baptise a child who does not understand it? We hope that as he grows, he will understand and that he himself will request Baptism." But this means not having confidence in the Holy Spirit, because when we baptise a child, the Holy Spirit enters that child, and the Holy Spirit cultivates in that child, from childhood, Christian values that will then flourish. This opportunity must always be given to everyone, to all children, to have within them the Holy Spirit who guides them during life. Do not forget to baptise your children!

No one can earn Baptism, which is always a gift freely given to all, adults and infants. But as happens for a seed full of life, this gift takes root and bears fruit in a soil nourished by faith. The baptismal promises that we renew each year in the Easter Vigil must be rekindled every day so that Baptism may "christify": we must not be afraid of this word; Baptism "christifies". Those who have received Baptism and are "christified"; they resemble Christ, are transformed in Christ and it truly renders them another Christ.

General Audience, 11th April 2018, St Peter's Square

The Sign of the Christian Faith

The significance of Baptism stands out clearly in its celebration; thus let us turn our attention to it. By considering the gestures and words of the liturgy we can understand the grace and the promise of this Sacrament, which is always to be rediscovered. We recall it in the sprinkling with holy water that can be done at the beginning of Mass on Sunday, as well as in the renewal of the baptismal promises during the Easter Vigil. In fact, as happens in the celebration of Baptism, a spiritual dynamic arises which passes through the entire life of the baptised; it is the beginning of a process that allows one to live united to Christ in the Church. Therefore, returning to the wellspring of Christian life leads us better to understand the gift received on the day of our Baptism and to renew our commitment to conform to it in the condition in which we find ourselves today. To renew our commitment, to better understand this gift which is Baptism, and to remember the day of our Baptism. Last Wednesday, as homework I asked that each of us remember the day of our Baptism, the day on which we were baptised. I know that some of you know it, others do not; those who do not know it, ask your family members, ask those people, godfathers, godmothers...: "What is the date of my Baptism?" Because Baptism is a rebirth and it is as if it were a second birthday. Do you understand? Do this homework; ask: "What is the date of my Baptism?"

First and foremost, in the Rite of Reception, the candidate's name is requested, because the name indicates a person's identity. When we introduce ourselves we say our name right away: "My name is...", so as to emerge from anonymity; an anonymous person is one who has no name. To emerge from anonymity we immediately say our name. Without a name one remains an outsider, without rights and duties. God calls each one by name, loving us individually, in the concreteness of our history. Baptism ignites the *personal* vocation to live as Christians, which will develop throughout our lifetime. And it entails a *personal* response, not taken on loan, with a "copy and paste". Christian life in fact is woven with a series of calls and responses: God continues to pronounce our name throughout the years, making his call to become conformed to his Son Jesus resonate in a thousand ways. Thus, one's name is important! It is very important! Parents think about the name to give to a child even before birth: this too is part of expecting a child who, in his own name, will have his original identity, also for the Christian life bound to God.

Of course, becoming Christian is a gift which comes from on high (cf. *Jn* 3:3-8). One cannot buy faith, but ask for it, yes; and receive it as a gift, yes. "Lord, give me the gift of faith" is a beautiful prayer! "That I may have faith" is a beautiful prayer. Asking for it as a gift, but it cannot be bought; it is asked for. Indeed, Baptism is "the sacrament of that faith by which, enlightened by the grace of the Holy Spirit, we respond to the Gospel of Christ" (*Christian Initiation*, General Introduction, n. 3). The *formation of catechumens* and the *preparation of parents*, as listening to the Word of

God in the very celebration of Baptism, tend to generate and reawaken a sincere faith in response to the Gospel.

Whereas adult catechumens personally manifest what they wish to receive as a gift from the Church, children are presented by their parents, with the godparents. The dialogue with them allows them to express the wish that the children receive Baptism and allows the Church to express the intention to celebrate it. "These purposes are expressed in action when the parents and the celebrant trace the sign of the cross on the foreheads of the children" (*Rite of Baptism for Children*, Introduction, n. 16). "The sign of the cross [...] marks with the imprint of Christ the one who is going to belong to him and signifies the grace of the redemption Christ won for us by his cross" (*Catechism of the Catholic Church*, n. 1235).

In the ceremony we make the sign of the Cross on the children. But I would like to return to a subject that I have talked to you about. Do our children know how to make the sign of the Cross properly? So often I have seen children who do not know how to make the sign of the Cross. And you, dads, mums, grandpas, grandmas, godfathers, godmothers, must teach them how to make the sign of the Cross properly, because it is repeating what was done in Baptism. Do you understand clearly? Teach children how to make the sign of the Cross. If they learn it as children they will do it well later, as grown-ups.

The Cross is the badge that shows who we are: our words, thoughts, gaze, works are under the sign of the Cross, that is, under the sign of Jesus's love to the very end. Children are marked on the forehead. Adult catechumens are also marked, on all their senses, with these words: "Receive the sign of the cross on your ears, that you may hear the voice of the Lord"; "Receive the sign of the cross on your eyes, that you may see the glory of God"; "Receive the sign of the cross on your lips, that you may respond to the word of God"; "Receive the sign of the cross over your heart, that Christ may dwell there by faith"; "Receive the sign of the cross on your shoulders, that you may bear the gentle yoke of Christ" (*Rite of Christian Initiation of Adults*", n. 85). We become Christians in the measure to which the Cross is imprinted on us as a "paschal" mark (cf. *Rev* 14:1; 22:4), making visible, also outwardly, the Christian way of confronting life. Making the sign of the Cross when we wake, before meals, in facing danger, to protect against evil, in the evening before we sleep, means telling ourselves and others whom we belong to, who we want to be. This is why it is so important to teach children how to make the sign of the Cross properly. And as we do upon entering a church, we can also do so at home, by keeping a bit of holy water in a suitable little vase – some families do so: this way, each time we come in or go out, by making the sign of the Cross with that water we remember that *we are baptised*. Do not forget, I repeat: teach the children how to make the sign of the Cross.

General Audience, 18th April 2018, St Peter's Square

The Strength to Overcome Evil

The Gospel enlightens the candidates and elicits the response of faith: "Indeed Baptism is 'the sacrament of faith' in a particular way, since it is the sacramental entry into the life of faith" (*Catechism of the Catholic Church*, n. 1236). And faith is the delivery of oneself to the Lord Jesus, recognised as "a spring of water [...] to eternal life" (*Jn* 4:14), "the light of the world" (*Jn* 9:5), "the resurrection and the life" (*Jn* 11:25), as taught by the path that catechumens approaching Christian initiation still take today. Instructed by listening to Jesus, his teachings and his work, the catechumens relive the experience of the Samaritan woman who thirsts for living water, the man born blind who opens his eyes to the light, Lazarus who walks out from the tomb. The Gospel has within it the power to transform those who accept it with faith, tearing them away from the control of the evil one so that they may learn to serve the Lord with joy and newness of life.

One never goes alone to the baptismal font, but is accompanied by the prayers of the entire Church, as recalled in the litanies of the saints which precede the Prayer of Exorcism and the Anointing Before Baptism, with which the catechumens are anointed with oil. These are gestures which, from antiquity, assure those who are preparing to be reborn as children of God that the prayers of the Church assist them in the battle against evil, accompany them on the path of good, help them elude the power of sin in order to enter into the kingdom of divine grace. The prayers of the Church. The Church prays, and prays for everyone, for all of us! We, the Church, pray for others. It is a beautiful thing to pray for others. Often, we have no urgent need and we do not pray. United to the Church, we must pray for others: "Lord I ask of you on behalf of those who are in need, on behalf of those who have no faith..." Do not forget: the Church's prayers are always in action. But we must enter into this prayer and pray for all the People of God and for those who need prayers. For this reason, the path of adult catechumens is marked by repeated exorcisms pronounced by the priest (cf. *Catechism of the Catholic Church*, n. 1237), that is, prayers which invoke liberation from sin and from everything which separates us from Christ and prevents intimate union with him. For children too, we ask God to free them from original sin and to consecrate their dwelling in the Holy Spirit (cf. *Rite of Baptism for Children*, n. 49). Children. Praying for children, for spiritual and corporeal health. It is a means of protecting children with prayer. As the Gospels attest, Jesus himself fought and cast out the demons to manifest the advent of the kingdom of God (cf. *Mt* 12:28): his victory over the power of the evil one leaves room for the Lordship of God who brings joy and reconciles with life.

Baptism is not a magical formula but a *gift of the Holy Spirit* who enables those who receive him to "fight against the spirit of evil", believing that God has sent his Son into the world to destroy the power of Satan and to transfer mankind from darkness into the kingdom of infinite light (cf. *Rite of Baptism for Children*, n. 49). We know from experience that Christian life is always subject to temptation, especially to the temptation to separate oneself from God, from his will, from communion with him, to fall again into the snares of worldly seductions. And Baptism prepares us. It gives us strength for this daily struggle, even for the battle against the devil who, as St Peter says, tries to devour us, to destroy us like a lion.

In addition to prayer, there is also the anointing of the breast of catechumens with oil: "it strengthens the candidates with the power to renounce the devil and sin before they go to the font of life for rebirth" (*Blessing of Oils and Chrism*, Introduction, n. 2). Due to the ability of oil to penetrate and benefit bodily tissues, combatants in ancient times would spread oil over their bodies to tone their muscles and to escape more easily from the grip of their adversary. In light of this symbolism, Christians in the early centuries adopted the use of anointing the bodies of baptismal candidates with oil blessed by the bishop[1] to show through this "sign of salvation" that the power of Christ the Saviour strengthens us to fight against evil and defeat it (*Rite of Baptism for Children*, n. 87).

---

[1] Here is the blessing prayer, expressive of the meaning of this oil: "O God, strength and protection of your people, who have made the oil you created a sign of strength, graciously bless this oil, and grant courage to the catechumens who will be anointed with it, so that, receiving divine wisdom and power, they may understand more deeply the Gospel of your Christ, they may undertake with a generous heart the labours of the Christian life, and, made worthy of adoption as your sons and daughters, they may rejoice to be born anew and to live in your Church." Blessing of the Oil of Catechumens (no.22)

It is tiring to fight against evil, to escape its deceit, to regain strength after an exhausting battle, but we must know that all of Christian life is a battle. We must also know, however, that we are not alone, that Mother Church prays so that her children, reborn in Baptism, do not succumb to the snares of the evil one but overcome them through the power of the Paschal Christ. Fortified by the Risen Christ who defeated the prince of this world (cf. *Jn* 12:31), we too can repeat with the faith of St Paul: "I can do all things in him who strengthens me" (*Phil* 4:13). We all can overcome, overcome anything, but with the strength that comes from Jesus.

General Audience, 25th April 2018, St Peter's Square

Source of Life

Continuing the reflection on Baptism, I would like to focus on the main rites, which take place at the baptismal font.

Let us consider first and foremost the water, on which the power of the Holy Spirit is invoked so that it may have the capacity to regenerate and renew (cf. *Jn* 3:5; *Tit* 3:5). Water is the matrix of life and wellbeing, whereas its absence causes all fruitfulness to die out, as happens in the desert. Water, however, can also be a cause of death, when one is submerged among its waves or when, in great quantity, it engulfs everything. Lastly, water has the capacity to wash, cleanse and purify.

Beginning with this natural, universally recognised symbolism, the Bible describes God's interventions and promises with the sign of water. However, the power to forgive sins does not lie in the water itself, as St Ambrose explained to the newly baptised: "You have seen the water, but water does not heal all things: healing water has the grace of Christ... The action is of the water, the effectiveness is of the Holy Spirit" (cf. *On the Sacraments*, 1:15).

For this reason the Church invokes the action of the Holy Spirit on the water so that all those "who are buried with Christ in the death of baptism" may rise again with him to eternal life (cf. *Rite of Baptism for Children*, 54). The prayer of the benediction says that God "made a sign of the waters of baptism" and recalls the principal biblical foreshadowing: the Spirit moved over the waters of creation to render them the seed of life (cf. *Gen* 1:1-2); the waters of the flood signalled the end of sin and the beginning of new life (cf. *Gen* 7:6-8, 22); through the waters of the Red Sea the children of Abraham were freed from slavery in Egypt (cf. *Ex* 14:15-31). In relation to Jesus, we recall his baptism in the Jordan (cf. *Mt* 3:13-17), the blood and water that poured from his side (cf. *Jn* 19:31-37), and the mandate to his disciples to baptise all peoples in the name of the Trinity (cf. *Mt* 28:19). Strengthened by this memory, we ask God to instil the water of the font with the grace of the dead and Risen Christ (cf. *Rite of Baptism for Children*, 54). And thus, this water is transformed into water that carries within it the power of the Holy Spirit. And with this water, with the power of the Holy Spirit, we baptise people, we baptise adults, children, everyone.

Once the water of the font has been blessed, the heart must be prepared to accept Baptism. This occurs with the renunciation of Satan and the Profession of Faith, two actions which are closely connected. In the same measure with which I say "no" to the suggestions of the devil – the one who divides – I am able to say "yes" to God who calls me to conform to him in thoughts and deeds. The devil divides. God always unites the community, mankind, into one single people. It is not possible to adhere to Christ by placing conditions. It is necessary to detach oneself from certain bonds in order truly to embrace others. One is either well with God or well with the devil. For this reason, the renunciation and the act of faith go together. It is necessary to burn some bridges, leaving them behind, in order to undertake the new Way which is Christ.

The response to the questions – "Do you renounce Satan, all his works and all his empty promises?" – is made in first person singular: "*I do*". And the profession of faith is made in the same way: "*I believe*". I renounce and I believe: this is the foundation of Baptism. It is a responsible choice which demands to be transformed into concrete gestures of trust in God. The act of faith assumes a commitment which Baptism itself will help to keep with perseverance in the various situations and trials of life. Let us recall the ancient wisdom of Israel: "My son, if you come forward to serve the Lord, prepare yourself for temptation" (*Sir* 2:1): that is, prepare yourself for battle. And the presence of the Holy Spirit gives us the strength to fight well.

Dear brothers and sisters, when we dip our hand into the blessed water – when entering a church, we touch the blessed water – and we make the sign of the Cross, let us think with joy and gratitude of the Baptism we received – this blessed water reminds us of Baptism – and let us renew our "Amen" – "I am happy" – in order to live immersed in the love of the most Holy Trinity.

General Audience, 2nd May 2018, St Peter's Square

Regeneration

The catechesis on the Sacrament of Baptism leads us to speak about the holy immersion accompanied by the invocation of the Holy Trinity, that is, the central rite, which actually "baptises" – that is, *immerses* – one in the Paschal Mystery of Christ (cf. *Catechism of the Catholic Church*, n. 1239). St Paul recalls the significance of this rite to the Christians of Rome, first asking: "Do you not know that all of us who have been baptised into Christ Jesus were baptised into his death?", and then responding: "We were buried [...] with him by baptism into death, so that as Christ was raised from the dead [...], we too might walk in newness of life" (*Rom* 6:4). Baptism opens for us the door to a life of resurrection, not to a worldly life. A life according to Jesus.

The baptismal font is the place in which one experiences the Easter Passover with Christ! The old man, with his "deceitful lusts" is buried (cf. *Eph* 4:22), so that a new creature may be born; truly the old things have passed away and new things are born (cf. *2 Cor* 5:17). The *Catechetical Lectures* attributed to St Cyril of Jerusalem thus explain to the newly baptised what has happened to them in the water of Baptism. This is St Cyril's beautiful explanation: "And at the self-same moment you were both dying and being born; and that water of salvation was at once your grave and your mother" (n. 20, *On the Mysteries*, ii, 4-6; pg 33, 1079-1082). The rebirth of the new man requires that the man corrupted by sin be reduced to dust. The images of the *tomb* and of the *maternal womb* referring to the font, indeed, clearly express what great things come about through the simple rite of Baptism. I like the inscription found on the ancient Roman Lateran Baptistry, which reads, in Latin, this expression attributed to Pope Sixtus III: "Mother Church conceives her offspring by the breath of God, and bears them virginally in this water. Hope for the Kingdom of Heaven, you who are reborn in this font".[2] It is beautiful: the Church that bears us, the Church which is womb, is our mother through Baptism.

If our parents have generated us in earthly life, the Church has regenerated us to eternal life in Baptism. We have become children in her Son Jesus (cf. *Rom* 8:15; *Gal* 4:5-7). Upon each one of us too, born anew through the water and through the Holy Spirit, the heavenly Father makes his voice resonate with infinite love, saying "You are my beloved son" (cf. *Mt* 3:17). This paternal voice, imperceptible to the ear but well audible to the heart of those who believe, accompanies us throughout our life, never abandoning us. Throughout our life the Father tells us: "You are my beloved son; you are my beloved daughter". God loves us so much, as a Father, and never forsakes us. It is so from the moment of Baptism. We are reborn as children of God for ever! Indeed, Baptism is not repeated, because it imprints an indelible spiritual seal: "No sin can erase this mark, even if sin prevents Baptism from bearing the fruits of salvation" (CCC, n. 1272).

---

[2] "*Virgineo fetu genitrix Ecclesia natos / quos spirante Deo concipit amne parit. / Caelorum regnum sperate hoc fonte renati*".

The seal of Baptism is never lost! "Father, but if a person becomes an infamous brigand, who kills people, who inflicts injustice, does the seal not disappear?" No. To his own shame a child of God is the person who does these things; but the seal does not go away. And he continues to be a child of God, who opposes God; but God never disowns his children. Do you understand this last point? God never disowns his children. Shall we all repeat it together? "God never disowns his children."

Incorporated in Christ through Baptism, the baptised are thus conformed to him, "the first-born son among many brethren" (*Rom* 8:29). Through the action of the Holy Spirit, Baptism purifies, sanctifies, justifies, to form in Christ, of many, one single body (*1 Cor* 6:11,12,13). The *chrismal anointing* "signifies the royal priesthood of the baptised and enrolment into the company of the people of God" (*Rite of Baptism for Children*, n. 18:3). Hence the priest anoints the head of every baptised person with the sacred chrism after pronouncing these words which explain the significance: God himself "anoints you with the chrism of salvation, so that, united with his people, you may remain for ever a member of Christ who is Priest, Prophet, and King" (*ibid*., n. 62). Brothers and sisters, here lies the entire Christian vocation: to live united to Christ in the holy Church, participants in the same consecration in order to carry out the same mission, in this world, bearing fruits that endure for ever. Enlivened by the One Spirit, in fact, the whole People of God participates in the offices of Jesus Christ, "Priest, Prophet and King", and "bears the responsibilities for mission and service that flow from them". (CCC, nn. 783-786).

What does it mean to participate in the royal and prophetic priesthood of Christ? It means making of oneself an offering acceptable to God (cf. *Rom* 12:1), bearing witness to him through a life of faith and charity (cf. *Lumen Gentium*, n. 12), placing it at the service of others, after the example of the Lord Jesus (cf. *Mt* 20:25-28; *Jn* 13:13-17). Thank you.

General Audience, 9th May 2018, St Peter's Square

Clothed with Christ

The spiritual effects of this Sacrament, invisible to the eye but active in the heart of one who has become a new creature, are clearly seen in the consignment of the white garment and the lighted candle.

After the washing of regeneration, capable of recreating the person in the likeness of God in true holiness (cf. *Eph* 4:24), since the first centuries, it has seemed natural to clothe the baptised in a *new white garment*, reflecting the splendour of life received in Christ and in the Holy Spirit. The white garment, while symbolically expressing what has occurred in the Sacrament, announces the condition of having been transfigured in divine glory.

St Paul recalls what it means to be clothed in Christ, when he explains *the virtues that the baptised must cultivate*: "put on, as God's chosen ones, holy and beloved, compassion, kindness, lowliness, meekness and patience, forbearing one another and [...] forgiving each other. And above all these, put on love, which binds everything together in perfect harmony" (cf. *Col* 3:12-14).

Even the ritual consignment of the *flame drawn from the Easter candle*, recalls the effect of Baptism: "Receive the light of Christ", says the priest. These words recall that we are not the light, but rather, the light is Jesus Christ (cf. *Jn* 1:9; 12:46), who, risen from the dead, overcame the shadows of evil. We are called to receive his splendour! As the flame of the Easter candle gives light to each single candle, so the love of the Risen Lord enflames the hearts of the baptised, filling them with light and warmth. And this is why, since the first centuries, Baptism has also been called "enlightenment", and the one who was baptised is called "enlightened".

This is indeed the Christian vocation: "Walk always as children of the light and keep the flame of faith alive in your hearts" (*Rite of Christian Initiation of Adults*, n. 321; cf. *Jn* 12:36). If children are involved, it is the duty of the parents, together with the godfathers and godmothers, to take care to nurture the flame of baptismal grace in their little ones, helping them persevere in the faith (cf. *Rite of Baptism for Children*, n. 100). Children have the right to Christian formation, which "seeks to lead them gradually to learn God's plan in Christ, so that they may ultimately accept for themselves the faith in which they have been baptised" (*ibid.*, Introduction, n. 3).

Christ's living presence, which is to be safeguarded, defended and expanded in us, is the lamp which lights our steps, the light which directs our choices, the flame which warms hearts on the journey to encounter the Lord, making us capable of helping those who journey with us, until the inseparable communion with him. From that day forth, Revelation also states, "night shall be no more; and they shall need no light of lamp or sun, for the Lord God will be their light, and they shall reign for ever and ever" (cf. 22:5).

The celebration of Baptism concludes with the prayer of the *Our Father*, which belongs to the community of the Children of God. Indeed, children reborn in Baptism will receive the gift of the Holy Spirit fulfilled in Confirmation and will participate in the Eucharist, learning what it means to address God by calling him "Father".

At the conclusion of these catecheses on Baptism, I repeat to each of you the invitation I thus expressed in the Apostolic Exhortation *Gaudete et Exsultate*: "Let the grace of your baptism bear fruit in a path of holiness. Let everything be open to God; turn to him in every situation. Do not be dismayed, for the power of the Holy Spirit enables you to do this, and holiness, in the end, is the fruit of the Holy Spirit in your life (cf. *Gal* 5:22-23)" (n. 15).

General Audience, 16th May 2018, St Peter's Square

CONFIRMATION

The Christian Witness

The Seal of the Spirit

For the Growth of the Church

The Christian Witness

After the catecheses on Baptism, the days which follow the Solemnity of Pentecost invite us to reflect on the witness that the Spirit inspires in the baptised, setting their life in motion, opening it to the good of others. Jesus entrusted a great mission to his disciples: "You are the salt of the earth; you are the light of the world" (cf. *Mt* 5:13-16). These are images that lead us to consider our behaviour, because both a lack and an excess of salt spoil the taste of food, just as a lack or an excess of light impede vision. Only the Spirit of Christ can truly become the salt that gives flavour and protects against corruption, and the light that illuminates the world! And this is the gift we receive in the Sacrament of Confirmation, or Chrismation, on which I would like to pause and reflect with you. It is called "*Confirmation*" because it confirms Baptism and strengthens its grace (cf. *Catechism of the Catholic Church*, n. 1289); and also "*Chrismation*", from the fact that we receive the Spirit through the anointing with "Chrism" (a fragrant oil mixture consecrated by the bishop), a term which refers to *Christ* anointed by the Holy Spirit.

The first step is being reborn to divine life in Baptism; it is important to behave as children of God, or to conform ourselves to Christ who works in the Holy Church, allowing us to engage in his mission in the world. This is what the anointing of the Holy Spirit foresees: "without his strength, man has nothing" (cf. Sequence for Pentecost). Without the power of the Holy Spirit we can do nothing:

it is the Spirit who gives us the power to go forth. As Jesus's entire life was enlivened by the Spirit, so too is the life of the Church and of each of her members under the guidance of the same Spirit.

Conceived by the Blessed Virgin by the power of the Holy Spirit, Jesus undertakes his mission after, having emerged from the water of the Jordan, he is consecrated by the Spirit who descends and remains upon him (cf. *Mk* 1:10; *Jn* 1:32). He proclaims this explicitly in the synagogue of Nazareth: it is beautiful how Jesus presents himself, which is Jesus's identity card in the synagogue of Nazareth! Let us hear how he does it: "The Spirit of the Lord is upon me, because he has anointed me to preach good news to the poor" (*Lk* 4:18). Jesus presents himself in the synagogue of his village as the Anointed One, the one who was anointed by the Holy Spirit.

Jesus is filled with the Holy Spirit and is the source of the Spirit promised by the Father (cf. *Jn* 15:26; *Lk* 24:49; *Acts* 1:8, 2:33). In reality, on the evening of Easter, the Risen One breathes on his disciples, saying to them: "Receive the Holy Spirit" (*Jn* 20:22); and on the Day of Pentecost the power of the Spirit descends upon the Apostles in an extraordinary form (cf. *Acts* 2:1-4), as we know.

The "Breath" of the Risen Christ fills the Church's lungs with life; and in effect the mouths of the disciples, "filled with the Holy Spirit", are opened in order to proclaim to all the great works of God (cf. *Acts* 2:1-11).

Pentecost – which we celebrated last Sunday – is for the Church what was for Christ the anointing of the Spirit received at the Jordan, that is, Pentecost is the missionary impulse to expend life for the sanctification of mankind, to the glory of God. If the Spirit works in every Sacrament, it is in a special way that in Confirmation "the faithful receive the Holy Spirit as a Gift" (Paul VI, Apostolic Constitution *Divinae Consortium Naturae*). And at the moment of anointing, the bishop says these words: "Be sealed with the Gift of the Holy Spirit": the Holy Spirit is God's great gift. And we all have the Spirit within. The Spirit is in our heart, in our soul. And the Spirit guides us in life so that we may become the true salt and the true light for mankind.

If in Baptism it is the Holy Spirit who immerses us in Christ, then in Confirmation it is Christ who fills us with his Spirit, consecrating us as his witnesses, participants in the same principle of life and of mission, according to the design of the heavenly Father. The witness given by the confirmed shows reception of the Holy Spirit and docility to his creative inspiration. I wonder: how can one see that we have received the Gift of the Spirit? If we fulfil the works of the Spirit, if we speak the words instructed by the Spirit (cf. *1 Cor* 2:13). Christian witness consists in doing only and all that the Spirit of Christ asks of us, giving us the strength to accomplish it.

General Audience, 23rd May 2018, St Peter's Square

The Seal of the Spirit

Continuing with the theme of Confirmation, or Chrismation, I would like to highlight "the intimate connection which this sacrament has with the whole of Christian initiation" (*Sacrosanctum Concilium*, n. 71).

Before receiving the spiritual anointing that confirms and strengthens the grace of Baptism, the confirmands are called to renew the promises made one day by their parents and godparents. Now they themselves profess the faith of the Church, ready to respond "I believe" to the questions asked by the bishop; ready, in particular, to believe "in the Holy Spirit, the Lord, the giver of life, who came upon the apostles at Pentecost and today is given to [them] sacramentally in confirmation" (*Rite of Confirmation* [RC], n. 23).

As the coming of the Holy Spirit requires hearts gathered in prayer (cf. *Acts* 1:14), after the silent prayer of the community, the bishop, extending his hands over the confirmands, asks God to instil in them his Holy Spirit Paraclete. There is only one Spirit (cf. *1 Cor* 12:4), but in coming to us he brings with him an abundance of gifts: wisdom, understanding, right judgement, courage, knowledge, reverence, and awe in the presence of God (cf. RC, n. 25). We have heard the Bible passage with these gifts which the Holy Spirit brings. According to the Prophet Isaiah (11:2), these are the seven virtues the Spirit poured out on the Messiah for the fulfilment of his mission. St Paul also describes the abundant fruits of the Spirit which are "love, joy, peace, patience, kindness, goodness, faithfulness, gentleness, self-control" (*Gal* 5:22). The one Spirit distributes the multiple gifts which enrich the one Church: he is the Author of diversity, but at the same time the Creator of unity. Thus the Spirit gives all these riches which, although different, create harmony, that is, the unity of all these spiritual riches that we Christians have.

Through the tradition established by the Apostles, the Spirit, who completes the grace of Baptism, is communicated through the laying on of hands (cf. *Acts* 8:15-17, 19:5-6; *Heb* 6:2). To this biblical gesture, to better express the outpouring of the Spirit which permeates those who receive it, early on an anointing with perfumed oil called chrism[3] was added, which is still in use today, in both the East and West (cf. *Catechism of the Catholic Church*, n. 1289).

The oil – chrism – is a therapeutic and cosmetic substance which by entering the bodily tissues medicates wounds and perfumes the limbs; because of these qualities it is used in biblical and liturgical symbolism to express the action of the Holy Spirit who consecrates and permeates the baptised, adorning them with charisms. The Sacrament

---

[3] Here is a passage of the prayer of Consecration of the Chrism: "Therefore we beseech you, Lord: be pleased to sanctify with your + blessing this oil in its richness, and to pour into it the strength of the Holy Spirit, with the powerful working of your Christ. From his holy name it has received the name of Chrism, and with it you have anointed your priests, prophets, kings, and martyrs." For those anointed with this chrism may it 'cleanse…the stain of their first birth' and make them 'temple[s] of your majesty…made fragrant with the innocence of a life pleasing to you.' (cf. Blessing of Oils and Chrism, n. 25).

is conferred through the anointing with chrism on the forehead, administered by the bishop by the imposition of his hand and with the words: "Be sealed with the Gift of the Holy Spirit".[4] The Holy Spirit is the invisible *gift* that is bestowed and the chrism is its visible *seal*.

In receiving on the forehead the sign of the Cross with fragrant oil, confirmands thus receive an indelible spiritual imprint, the "character", which conforms them more perfectly to Christ and gives them the grace to spread the "good aroma" among men (cf. *2 Cor* 2:15).

Let us listen again to St Ambrose's invitation to the newly confirmed. He said: "recollect that you have received the spiritual seal [...] and preserve what you have received. God the Father has sealed you, Christ the Lord has confirmed you, and has given the earnest of the Spirit in your heart" (*On the Mysteries*, 7:42; CSEL 73:106; cf. CCC, n. 1303). The Holy Spirit is an unmerited gift, to be received with gratitude, making room for his boundless creativity. It is a gift to be safeguarded with care, yielded to with docility, allowing oneself to be moulded, like wax, by the warmth of his charity, so as to "reflect Jesus Christ in today's world" (Apostolic Exhortation *Gaudete et Exsultate*, n. 23).

General Audience, 30th May 2018, St Peter's Square

---

[4] The phrases "Receive the Holy Spirit" and "the gift of the Holy Spirit" are found in *Jn* 20:22, and *Acts* 2:38, 10:45-47.

For the Growth of the Church

Let us consider the effects that the gift of the Holy Spirit ripens in the newly confirmed, leading them to become, in their turn, a gift to others. The Holy Spirit is a gift. Let us remember that when the bishop anoints us with the oil he says: "Receive the gift of the Holy Spirit". That gift of the Holy Spirit enters us and makes us fruitful, so that we can then give him to others. Receiving is always for giving: never receive and keep things within, as if the soul were a storehouse. No: receiving is always for giving. God's grace is received to be given to others. This is the life of a Christian. Indeed it pertains to the Holy Spirit who shifts us from our "I" in order to open us up to the "we" of the community: receiving in order to give. We are not at the centre: we are an instrument of that gift for others.

Completing the likeness to Christ in those who are baptised, Confirmation *unites them more closely as living members to the mystical body of the Church* (cf. *Rite of Confirmation*, n. 22). The Church's mission in the world proceeds through the contribution of all those who are part of her. Some think there are bosses in the Church: the Pope, the bishops, the priests, and then there are the others. No: the Church is all of us! And we all have the responsibility to sanctify one another, to take care of the others. The Church is all of us. Each one has his or her work in the Church, but she is all of us. Indeed, we should think of the Church as a living organism, made up of people we know and with whom we journey, and not as an abstract and distant reality. The Church is we who are journeying; the Church is we who are in this Square today. Us: this is the Church. Confirmation binds us to the universal Church spread throughout the world, at the same time, actively involving confirmands in the life of the particular Church to which they belong, with the bishop, who is the successor of the Apostles, at the helm.

This is why the bishop is the *original minister* of Confirmation (cf. *Lumen Gentium*, n. 26), because he introduces the confirmand into the Church. The fact that in the Latin Church this Sacrament is usually conferred by the bishop demonstrates clearly that "its effect is to unite those who receive it more closely to the Church, to her apostolic origins, and to her mission of bearing witness to Christ" (*Catechism of the Catholic Church*, n. 1313).

This ecclesial incorporation is well demonstrated by the sign of peace which concludes the Rite of Confirmation. Indeed the bishop says to each confirmand: "Peace be with you". Recalling Christ's greeting to the disciples on the evening of Easter, filled with the Holy Spirit (cf. *Jn* 20:19-23) – as we have heard – these words illuminate a gesture which "demonstrates ecclesial communion with the bishop and with all the faithful" (cf. CCC, n. 1301). In Confirmation, we receive the Holy Spirit and peace: that peace that we must give to others. But let us think: each one think of his or her own parish community, for example. There is the ceremony of Confirmation, and then we offer each other peace: the bishop offers it to the confirmand, and then in the Mass, we exchange it among ourselves. This signifies harmony; it signifies charity among us; it signifies peace. But then what happens?

We go out and begin to speak ill of others, to "excoriate" others. Gossip begins. And gossip is war. This will not do! If we have received the sign of peace with the power of the Holy Spirit, we must be men and women of peace, and not destroy, with the tongue, the peace that the Holy Spirit has created. Poor Holy Spirit: the work we give him, with this habit of gossiping! Think carefully: gossip is not the work of the Holy Spirit; it is not the work of unity in the Church. Gossip destroys what God has made. Please: let us stop gossiping!

Confirmation is received only once, but the spiritual dynamism inspired by the holy anointing perseveres over time. We will never finish fulfilling the mandate to diffuse everywhere the good fragrance of a holy life, inspired by the fascinating simplicity of the Gospel.

No one receives Confirmation for himself alone, but to co-operate in the spiritual growth of others. Only in this way, by opening and coming out of ourselves to meet our brothers and sisters, can we truly grow and not merely delude ourselves we are doing so. In fact, what we receive as the gift of God must be given – the gift is to be given – in order to be fruitful, and not instead buried due to selfish fears, as the Parable of the Talents teaches (cf. *Mt* 25:14-30). The seed too: when we have the seed in hand, it is to be sown, not put away, in the dresser, to be left there. We have to give the gift of the Holy Spirit to the community. I exhort confirmands not to "confine" the Holy Spirit, not to resist the Wind that blows, that pushes them to walk in freedom; not to smother the ardent Fire of charity that leads one to expend one's life for God and for brothers and sisters. May the Holy Spirit grant to all of us the apostolic courage to communicate the Gospel, in deed and word, to those we meet on our way. With deeds and words, but good words: those which build up. Not the words of gossip, which destroy. Please, when you leave the church, consider that the peace received is to be given to others: not for destroying with gossip. Do not forget this.

General Audience, 6th June 2018, St Peter's Square

The Ten Commandments

Introduction: The Desire for a Full Life

Today, we shall begin a new series of catecheses on the theme of the Commandments. The Commandments of the Law of God. To introduce it, let us draw from the passage just heard: the encounter between Jesus and a man – he is a young man – who, on his knees, asks Jesus how he can inherit eternal life (cf. *Mk* 10:17-21). And in that question is the challenge of every life, ours too: the desire for a full, infinite life. What must we do to achieve it? What path must we take? To truly live, to live a noble life... How many young people try to "*live*" and destroy themselves by following things that are fleeting.

Some think that it would be better to extinguish this impulse – the impulse to live – because it is dangerous. I would like to say, especially to young people: our worst enemy is not practical problems, no matter how serious and dramatic: life's greatest danger is a poor spirit of adaptation which is neither meekness nor humility, but *mediocrity, cowardice.*[5] Is a mediocre young person a youth with a future or not? No! He or she remains there, will not grow, will not have success. Mediocrity or cowardice. Those young people who are afraid of everything: "No, this is how I am..." These young people will not move forward. Meekness, strength, and not cowardice, not mediocrity.

---

[5] The Fathers speak of cowardice (oligopsychìa). St John Damascene defines it as "the fear of completing an action" (*Exact Exposition of the Orthodox Faith*, ii, 15) and St John Climacus adds that "cowardice is a childish disposition, in an old, vainglorious soul" (*Ladder of Divine Ascent*, xxi, 2).

Blessed Pier Giorgio Frassati – he was a young man – used to say that one must live, not just get by.[6] The mediocre just get by, living by their life force. One must ask the heavenly Father, for today's young people, for the gift of a healthy *restlessness*. But, at home, in your homes, in every family, when a young person is seen sitting idle all day, at times mum and dad wonder: "Is he sick; is something wrong?", and they take him to the doctor. The life of young people is about moving forward, being restless, healthy restlessness, the capacity not to be content with a life without beauty, without colour. If young people are not hungry for an authentic life, I wonder, where will humanity end up? Where will humanity go with young people who are idle and not restless?

The question of that man in the Gospel passage that we have heard is inside of each of us: how can we find life, life in abundance, happiness? Jesus answers: "*You know the commandments*" (v. 19), and cites part of the Ten Commandments. It is a pedagogical process, by which Jesus wishes to lead to an exact place; in fact it is already clear, from that man's question, that he does not have a full life; he seeks more and is restless. Thus, what does he need in order to understand? He says: "Teacher, all these I have observed from my youth" (v. 20).

How do we pass from *youth* to *maturity*? When we begin to *accept our own limitations*. We become adults when we "relativise" and become aware of "what is lacking" (cf. v. 21). This man is forced to acknowledge that everything he

---

6 Cf. Letter to Isidoro Bonini, 27th February 1925.

is able to "do" does not rise above a "ceiling"; it does not cross a border.

How great it is to be men and women! How precious our existence is! Yet, there is a truth that, in the history of the last centuries, mankind has often rejected, with tragic consequences: the truth of our limitations.

In the Gospel Jesus says something that can help us: "Think not that I have come to abolish the law and the prophets; I have come not to abolish them but to *fulfil them*" (*Mt* 5:17). The Lord Jesus gives us the fulfilment; he came for this. That man had to come to the brink, where he had to take a decisive leap, where the possibility was presented to stop living for himself, for his own deeds, for his own goods and – precisely because he lacked a full life – to leave everything to follow the Lord.[7] Clearly, in Jesus's final – immense, wonderful – invitation, there is no proposal of poverty, but of wealth, of the true richness: "*You lack one thing; go, sell what you have, and give to the poor, and you will have treasure in heaven; and come, follow me*" (*Mk* 10:21).

Being able to choose between an original and a copy, who would choose the copy? Here is the challenge: finding life's original, not the copy. Jesus does not offer surrogates, but *true* life, *true* love, *true* richness! How will young people be able to follow us in faith if they do not see us choose the original, if they see us adjusting to half measures? It is awful to find half-measure Christians – allow me the

7 "The eye was created for light, the ear for sounds, each thing for its particular purpose, and the desire of the soul for soaring toward Christ" (Nicholas Cabasilas, *The Life in Christ*, ii, 90).

word, "dwarf" Christians; they grow to a certain height and no more; Christians with a miniaturised, closed heart. It is awful to find this. We need the example of someone who invites me to a "*beyond*", a "*plus*", to grow a little. St Ignatius called it the "*magis*", "the fire, the fervour of action that rouses us from slumber".[8]

The path of what is lacking passes through what there is. Jesus did not come to abolish the Law nor the prophets, but to fulfil them. We must start from reality in order to take the leap into "*what we lack*". We must scrutinise the ordinary in order to open ourselves to the extraordinary.

In these catecheses we will take the two tablets of Moses as Christians, taking Jesus's hand, in order to pass from the illusions of youth to the treasure that is in heaven, walking behind him. We will discover, in each of these laws, ancient and wise, the door opened by the Father who is in heaven so that the Lord Jesus, who has crossed the threshold, may lead us to true life. His life. The life of the children of God.

General Audience, 13th June 2018, St Peter's Square

---

[8] Address to the 36th General Congregation of the Society of Jesus, 24th October 2016: "It is a magis, that plus that leads Ignatius to undertake initiatives, to follow them through, and to evaluate their real impact on peoples' lives in matters of faith, justice, mercy, and charity".

"Ten Words" to Live the Covenant

In the Introduction we saw that the Lord Jesus did not come to abolish the Law but to fulfil it. But we need to understand this perspective better.

In the Bible the Commandments do not exist for themselves, but are *part of a rapport, a relationship*. The Lord Jesus did not come to abolish the Law but to fulfil it. And there is that relationship, the *Covenant*[9] *between God and his people*. At the beginning of chapter 20 of the Book of Exodus we read – and this is important – "*God spoke all these words*" (v. 1).

It seems to be an introduction like any other, but nothing in the Bible is banal. The text does not say: "*God spoke these commandments*", but "*these words*". Jewish tradition will always call the Decalogue "the Ten Words".

[9] Chapter 20 of the Book of Exodus is preceded by the offer of the Covenant in chapter 19, in which the pronouncement is central: "Now therefore, if you will obey my voice and keep my covenant, you shall be my own possession among all peoples; for all the earth is mine, and you shall be to me a kingdom of priests and a holy nation" (*Ex* 19:5-6). This terminology is emblematically summarised in Lev 26:12: "I will walk among you, and will be your God, and you shall be my people", and continues up to the announcement of the name of the Messiah, foretold in Isaiah 7:14, that is, Emmanuel, which appears in Matthew: "Behold, a virgin shall conceive and bear a son, and his name shall be called Emmanuel (which means, God with us)" (*Mt* 1:23). All this indicates the essentially relational nature of the Jewish faith and, to the greatest degree, the Christian faith.

And this is exactly what the term "decalogue" means.[10] Yet they have the form of laws; they are objectively commandments. Why, then, does the sacred Author use, precisely here, the term "ten words"? Why? Why does he not say "ten commandments"?

Is there a difference between a *command* and a *word*? A command is a communication that does not require dialogue. A word, instead, is the essential medium of *relationship as a dialogue*. God the Father creates by means of his Word, and his Son is the Word made flesh. Love is nourished by words, and likewise education or co-operation. Two people who do not love each other are unable to communicate. When someone speaks to our heart, our loneliness is over. It receives a word; there is communication, and the commandments are God's words: God communicates through these ten Words, and he awaits our response.

It is one thing to receive an order, and quite another to perceive that someone is trying to speak to us. A dialogue is much more than the communication of a truth. I may say to you: "Today is the last day of Spring, warm Spring, but today is the last day." This is a truth; it is not a dialogue. But if I ask you: "What do you think about this Spring?", a dialogue begins. The Commandments are a dialogue. Communication "arises from the enjoyment of speaking and it enriches those who express their love for one another through the medium of words. This is an enrichment which does not consist in objects but in persons who share

---

[10] Cf. also *Ex* 24:28b: "he wrote upon the tables the words of the covenant, the ten commandments".

themselves in dialogue" (Apostolic Exhortation *Evangelii Gaudium*, n. 142).

But this difference is not something artificial. We see what happened in the beginning. The Tempter, the devil, wants to deceive man and woman on this point: he wants to convince them that God has forbidden them to eat the fruit of the tree of [the knowledge of] good and evil in order to keep them submissive. This is precisely the challenge: is the first rule that God gave to man a despot's imposition which forbids and compels, or is it the care of a father who is looking after his little ones and protecting them from self-destruction? Is it a word or a command? The most tragic among the various lies that the serpent tells Eve is the insinuation of an envious divinity – "But no, God envies you" – of a possessive divinity – "God does not want you to be free". The facts show dramatically that the serpent has lied (cf. *Gen* 2:16-17; 3:4-5); he made believe that a loving word was a command.

Man is at this crossroads: does God impose things on me or does he take care of me? Are his commandments merely a law or do they contain a word, to nurture me? Is God master or Father? God is Father: never forget this. Even in the worst situations, remember that we have a Father who loves us all. Are we subjects or children? This battle, inside and outside of us, is constantly present: a thousand times we have to choose between a slavish mentality and the mentality of children. A commandment is from the master; a word is from the Father.

The Holy Spirit is a Spirit of children; he is the Spirit of Jesus. A spirit of slaves cannot but view the Law as oppressive, and this can produce two conflicting results: either a life made up of duties and obligations, or a violent reaction of rejection. The whole of Christianity is the passage from the letter of the Law to the life-giving Spirit (cf. *2 Cor* 3:6-17). Jesus is the Word of the Father; he is not the condemnation of the Father. Jesus came to save, with his Word, not to condemn us.

One sees whether a man or a woman has lived this transition or not. People realise whether a Christian reasons as a Christian or as a slave. And we ourselves remember if our teachers took care of us like fathers and mothers, or if they only imposed rules. The Commandments are the journey toward freedom. They set us free because they are the Word of the Father on this journey.

The world needs not legalism but care. It needs Christians with the heart of children.[11] It needs Christians with the heart of children: do not forget this.

General Audience, 20th June 2018, St Peter's Square

---

[11] Cf. John Paul II, Encyclical Letter *Veritatis Splendor*, n. 12: "The gift of the Decalogue was a promise and sign of the New Covenant, in which the law would be written in a new and definitive way upon the human heart (cf. *Jer* 31:31-34), replacing the law of sin which had disfigured that heart (cf. *Jer* 17:1). In those days, 'a new heart' would be given, for in it would dwell 'a new spirit', the Spirit of God (cf. *Ez* 36:24-28)".

The Love of God Precedes the Law and Gives it Meaning

The Commandments, as we have said, more than commandments are the words of God to his people to help them journey properly, obeying the Father's loving words.

The Ten Words begin in this way: "*I am the Lord your God, who brought you out of the land of Egypt, out of the house of bondage*" (*Ex* 20:2). This beginning would seem foreign to the true and proper laws that follow. But it is not so.

Why does God make this proclamation about himself and about liberation? Because one reaches Mount Sinai after having crossed the Red Sea: the God of Israel first saves, then asks for trust.[12] In other words: the Decalogue begins from God's generosity. God never asks without giving first. First he saves; first he gives; then he asks. Such is our Father: a good God.

---

[12] In rabbinic tradition there is an enlightening text on the matter: "Why were the ten words not proclaimed at the beginning of the Torah? ... To what can they be compared? A man, taking on the governing of a city, asked its inhabitants: 'May I govern you?' But they answered: 'What good have you done that you would claim to govern us?' So, what did he do? He built them a protective wall and channels to provide water for the city; then he fought wars for them. And when he asked again: 'May I govern you?', they answered, 'Yes, yes.' Just as the Lord made Israel leave Egypt, split the sea for them, made manna descend for them and water rise from the well, brought them quails flying and lastly fought the war against Amalek for them. And when he asked them: 'May I govern you?', they answered: 'Yes, yes'" ('The gift of the Torah, Commentary on the Decalogue of Ex 20' in R. Ishmael's Mekilta, Rome, 1982, p. 49).

Let us understand the importance of the first declaration: "*I am the Lord, your God*". There is a possessive; there is a relationship; there is belonging. God is not extraneous: he *is your God.*[13] This illuminates the entire Decalogue and also reveals the secret of Christian action, because it is the very same attitude of Jesus, who says: "*As the Father has loved me, so have I loved you*" (*Jn* 15:9). Christ is loved by the Father, and he loves us with that love. He puts not himself but the Father first. Often our deeds fail because we put ourselves and not gratitude first. And one who begins with himself: where does he end up? He ends up with himself! He is incapable of making headway; he turns in on himself. It is precisely this selfish attitude that, in jest, people say: "That person is just I; me; with me and for me." He begins and ends with himself.

Christian life is above all the *grateful response* to a generous Father. Christians who only fulfil their "*duties*" do not have a personal experience with that God who is "*ours*". I must do this, this, that... Only duties. But you lack something! What is the foundation of this duty? The foundation of this duty is the love of God the Father, who gives first, then commands.

[13] Cf. Benedict XVI, Encyclical Letter *Deus Caritas Est*, 17: "The love-story between God and man consists in the very fact that this communion of will increases in a communion of thought and sentiment, and thus our will and God's will increasingly coincide: God's will is no longer for me an alien will, something imposed on me from without by the commandments, but it is now my own will, based on the realisation that God is in fact more deeply present to me than I am to myself. Then self-abandonment to God increases and God becomes our joy".

Placing the law before the relationship does not help the journey of faith. How can a young person want to be Christian, if we start with obligations, responsibilities, consistency and not with liberation? But being Christian is a journey of liberation! The Commandments free you from your selfishness and free you because it is God's love that leads you forward. Christian formation is not based on willpower, but on the acceptance of salvation, on letting oneself be loved: first the Red Sea, then Mount Sinai. First salvation: God saves his people in the Red Sea; then on Sinai he tells them what they have to do. But those people know that they are doing these things because they have been saved by a Father who loves them.

Gratitude is a characteristic of a heart that has been visited by the Holy Spirit. In order to obey God, it is above all necessary to remember his benefits. St Basil says: "Those who do not let such benefits fall into disregard orient themselves towards good virtue and towards all works of justice" (*Shorter Rules*, 56). Where does all this take us? To perform a memory exercise:[14] how many wonderful things God has done for each of us! How generous our heavenly Father is! I would now like to propose a small exercise in silence. Each can answer in his or her own heart. How many beautiful things has God done for me? This is the question. Let each of us reply in silence. How many beautiful things has God done for me? And this is the liberation of God. God does many beautiful things and he frees us.

---

[14] Cf. Homily in the Domus Sanctae Marthae, 7th October 2014: "What is prayer? It means remembering our history, before God. Because our history" is "the history of his love for us", 10th October 2014, p. 17; cf. *Detti e fatti dei padri del deserto*, Milan 1975, p. 71: "Disregard is the root of all evil".

And yet some may feel that they have not yet truly experienced God's liberation. This can happen. It may be that one looks inside oneself and finds only a sense of duty, a spirituality of servants, not of sons and daughters. What should be done in this case? As the Chosen People did. The Book of Exodus reads: "And the people of Israel groaned under their bondage, and cried out for help, and their cry under bondage came up to God. And God heard their groaning, and God remembered his covenant with Abraham, with Isaac, and with Jacob. And God saw the people of Israel, and God knew their condition" (*Ex* 2:23-25). God thinks of me.

God's liberating action placed at the beginning of the Decalogue – that is, the Commandments – is the response to this groaning. We do not save ourselves on our own, but a cry for help can escape us: "Lord save me; Lord teach me the way; Lord caress me; Lord give me some joy." This is a *cry for help*. It is up to us to ask to be liberated from selfishness, from sin, from the chains of slavery. This cry is important. It is prayer; it is being conscious of what is still oppressed and not liberated within us. There are many things fettered in our soul. "Save me; help me; set me free." This is a beautiful prayer to the Lord. God awaits that cry because he can and wants to break our chains. God did not call us to life to remain oppressed but rather to be free and to live in gratitude, obeying with joy the One who has given us so much, infinitely more than we could ever give to him. This is beautiful. May God always be blessed for all that he has done, does and will do within us!

General Audience, 27th June 2018, St Peter's Square

"You will not have other gods besides me"

We have heard the first commandment of the Decalogue: "You shall have no other gods besides me" (*Ex* 20:3). It is good to pause on the theme of *idolatry* which is significant and timely.

The commandment bans us from setting up idols[15] or images[16] of any kind of reality.[17] Indeed, everything can be used as an idol. We are speaking about a human tendency that involves both believers and atheists. For example, we Christians can ask ourselves: who is truly my God? Is it the One and Triune Love or is it my image, my personal success, perhaps even within the Church? "Idolatry not only refers to false pagan worship. It remains a constant temptation to faith. Idolatry consists in divinising what is not God" (*Catechism of the Catholic Church*, n. 2113).

What is a "god" on the existential plane? It is what is at the centre of one's life and on whom one's actions and

---

[15] The term Pesel means "a divine image originally sculpted in wood or stone and mostly in metal" (L. Koehler, W. Baumgartner, *The Hebrew and Aramaic Lexicon of the Old Testament*, vol. 3. p. 949).

[16] The term Temunah has a very broad meaning which can be reduced to a "likeness, form"; thus the ban is very broad and these images can be of any kind (cf. L. Koehler, W. Baumgartner, op. cit., vol. 1, p. 504).

[17] The command does not ban images per se – God himself ordered Moses to make golden cherubs on the cover of the Ark (cf. *Ex* 25:18) and a bronze serpent (cf. *Num* 21:8), but he bans these from being worshipped and served, thus the entire process of deification of something, not just its reproduction.

thoughts depend.[18] One can grow up in a family that is Christian in name but that is actually centred on reference points that are foreign to the Gospel.[19] Human beings cannot live without being centred on something. And so the world offers the "supermarket" of idols, which can be objects, images, ideas and roles. For example, even prayer. We must pray to God, our Father. I remember one day I had gone to a parish in the Diocese of Buenos Aires to celebrate Mass and after that, I had to celebrate Confirmation in another parish that was a kilometre away. I went on foot and I walked across a beautiful park. But in that park, there were over fifty tables with two chairs each, and people were seated facing each other. What were they doing? Tarot cards. They went there "to pray" to their idol. Instead of praying to God who is the providence of the future, they went there to have their fortunes told, to see the future. This is one form of the idolatry of our times. I ask you: how many of you have gone to have your cards read to see the future? How many of you, for example, have gone to have your hands read to see the future instead of praying to the Lord? This is the difference: the Lord is alive. The others are idols, forms of idolatry that are unnecessary.

---

[18] The Hebrew Bible refers to Canaanite idolatry with the term Ba'al which means "lordship, intimate relationship, reality on which one depends". The idol is domineering, takes the heart and becomes a pivot of life (cf. *Theological Lexicon of the Old Testament*, vol. 1, 257-251).

[19] Cf. *Catechism of the Catholic Church*, n. 2114: "Idolatry is a perversion of man's innate religious sense. An idolater is someone who 'transfers his indestructible notion of God to anything other than God' (Origen, *Contra Celsum*, 2, 40)".

How does idolatry develop? The commandment describes the various phases: "You shall not make for yourself a graven image or any likeness [...] you shall not bow down to them or serve them" (*Ex* 20:4-5).

The word "*idol*" in Greek is derived from the verb "*to see*".[20] An idol is a "*vision*" which has the tendency to become a fixation, an obsession. The idol in reality is a projection of self onto objects or projects. Advertising, for example, uses this dynamic: I cannot see the object itself but I can perceive that car, that smartphone, that role – or other things – as a means of fulfilling myself and responding to my basic needs. And I seek it out, I speak of it, I think of it: the idea of owning that object or fulfilling that project, reaching that position, seems a marvellous path to happiness, a tower with which to reach the heavens (cf. *Gen* 11:1-19), and then everything serves that goal.

We then enter the second phase: "*You shall not bow down to them*". Idols need worship, certain rituals: one bows down and sacrifices everything to them. In ancient times, there were human sacrifices to idols, but today too: children are sacrificed for a career, or neglected, or, quite simply, not conceived. Beauty demands human sacrifices. How many hours are spent in front of the mirror! How much do some people, some women, spend on makeup? This too is idolatry. It is not bad to wear makeup but in a normal way, not to become a goddess. Beauty demands human sacrifices. Fame demands the immolation of self,

---

[20] The etymology of the Greek eidolon, derived from eidos is from the root word weid which means to see (cf. *Grande Lessico dell'Antico Testamento*, Brescia 1967, vol. iii, p. 127).

of one's innocence and authenticity. Idols demand blood. Money robs one of life, and pleasure leads to loneliness. Economic structures sacrifice human life for greater profit. Let us think of unemployed people. Why? Because at times the businessmen of that company, of that firm, have decided to lay off those people in order to earn more money. The idol of money. We live in hypocrisy, doing and saying what others expect because the god of one's self affirmation imposes it. And lives are ruined, families are destroyed and young people are left prey to destructive models in order to increase profit. Drugs too are idols. How many young people ruin their health, even their lives, by worshipping the idol of drugs?

And here we come to the third and most tragic phase: and *you shall not serve them*, he says. Idols enslave. They promise happiness but do not deliver it and we find ourselves living for that thing or that vision, drawn into a self-destructive vortex, waiting for a result that never comes.

Dear brothers and sisters, idols promise life, but in reality they take it away. The true God does not demand life but gives it, as a gift. The true God does not offer a projection of our success but teaches us how to love. The true God does not demand children but gives his Son for us. Idols project future hypotheses and make us despise the present. The true God teaches how to live in everyday reality, in a practical way, not with illusions about the future: today and tomorrow and the day after tomorrow, walking towards the future; the concreteness of the true God against the fluidity of idols. Today, I invite you to think: how many idols do I have and which one is my favourite? Because recognising one's own forms of idolatry is the beginning of grace and puts one on the path of love. Indeed, love is incompatible with idolatry. If something becomes absolute and supreme, then it is more important than a spouse, than a child or a friendship. Being attached to an object or an idea makes one blind to love. And so, in order to pursue idols, one idol, one can even renounce a father, a mother, children, a wife, a husband, a family...the dearest things of all. Being attached to an object or an idea makes us blind to love. Take this to heart: idols rob us of love, idols make us blind to love and, in order to truly love, we must be free from all idols.

What is my idol? Remove it and throw it out of the window!

General Audience, 1st August 2018, St Peter's Square

Idolatry

Let us look more closely at the theme of *idolatry*. Now let us take up the theme again because it is very important to know about it. And, let us take our cue from the idol *par excellence*, the golden calf, which the Book of Exodus (32:1-8) describes – we have just heard a passage from it. This episode has a precise context: the desert where the people await Moses who has gone up the mountain to receive God's instructions.

What is *the desert*? It is a place where uncertainty and insecurity reign – there is nothing in the desert – where there is no water, no food and no shelter. The desert is an image of human life, whose condition is uncertain and has no inviolable guarantees. This insecurity creates a primal anxiety in mankind which Jesus mentions in the Gospel: "What shall we eat? What shall we drink? What shall we wear?" (*Mt* 6:31). These are primal anxieties. And the desert causes these anxieties.

And something occurs in that desert which triggers idolatry. "Moses delayed to come down from the mountain" (*Ex* 32:1). He remained there for forty days and the people grew impatient. The reference point was missing: Moses, the leader, the one in charge, the reassuring guide; and this became unbearable. Thus, the people called for a visible god – this is the snare into which the people fell – in order to identify and orient themselves. And they said to Aaron: "make us gods, who shall go before us" (v. 1); make us a leader, make us a chief. In order to escape uncertainty –

the uncertainty is the desert – human nature seeks a do-it-yourself religion. If God does not show himself, then we custom-make one for ourselves. "Before an idol, there is no risk that we will be called to abandon our security, for idols 'have mouths, but they cannot speak' (*Ps* 115:5). Idols exist, we begin to see, as a pretext for setting ourselves at the centre of reality and worshipping the work of our own hands" (*Lumen Fidei*, 13).

Aaron is unable to refuse the people's request, and he makes a *golden calf*. The calf had a double meaning in the ancient Near East: on the one hand it represented fertility and abundance, and on the other, energy and strength. But first and foremost, it was golden, thus, a symbol of wealth, success, power and money. These are the great idols: success, power and money. They are timeless temptations! This is what the golden calf is: the symbol of all desires that give the illusion of freedom but instead enslave, because an idol always enslaves; it has charm and you succumb; the charm of the serpent who looks at the little bird and the bird is unable to move, and the serpent gets him. Aaron was unable to refuse.

But above all, everything stems from the inability to confide in God, to place our insecurities in him, to allow him to give true depth to the desires of our hearts. This also allows us to sustain weakness, uncertainty and precariousness. Referring to God makes us strong in weakness, in uncertainty and also in precariousness. Without God's primacy one can easily fall into idolatry and settle for poor reassurances. But this is a temptation which we always read about in the Bible. And consider this carefully: it did not cost God much effort to free the people from Egypt: he did so with signs of power, of love. But God's great work was to remove Egypt from the hearts of the people, that is, to remove idolatry from the people's hearts. And again, God continues to work to remove it from our hearts. This is God's great work: to remove "that Egypt" which we carry within us, which is the attraction of idolatry.

When we welcome the God of Jesus Christ who was rich and became poor for us (cf. *2 Cor* 8:9), then we discover that recognising one's weaknesses is not a disgrace of human life, but the condition necessary to open up to the One who is truly strong. Thus, God's salvation enters through the door of weakness (cf. *2 Cor* 12:10). It is due to man's own inadequacies that he opens up to the paternity of God. Mankind's *freedom* comes from allowing the true God to be the only Lord, and this allows one to *accept one's fragility* and *reject the idols in one's heart*.

We Christians turn our gaze to *Christ crucified* (cf. *Jn* 19:37) who was weak, insulted and stripped of all his possessions. But the face of the true God is revealed in him, the true glory of love and not that of glittering deceit. Isaiah says: "he was wounded by our transgressions" (*Is* 53:5). We were healed by the very weakness of a man who was God, by his wounds. And through our weaknesses, we can open up to God's salvation. Our healing comes from the One who became poor, who welcomed failure, who undertook to bear our insecurity until the end, in order to fill it with love and strength. He comes to reveal God's paternity to us. In Christ our fragility is no longer a curse but a place of encounter with the Father and the wellspring of a new strength from above.

General Audience, 8th August 2018, St Peter's Square

Respect the Name of the Lord

Let us focus on the Commandment "*You shall not take the name of the Lord your God in vain*" (*Ex* 20:7). We rightly interpret these words as an invitation not to offend the name of God and to avoid using it inappropriately. This clear meaning prepares us for a more in-depth look at these precious words: not to take the name of God inappropriately or in vain.

Let us listen to them more closely. The precept "you shall not take" translates an expression which, both in Hebrew and in Greek, literally means "*you shall not take upon yourself, you shall not assume*".

The expression "in vain" is clearer and means "*idly, vainly*". It refers to an empty casing, a form that has no content. It is a trait of hypocrisy, of formality and lies and of using words or the name of God, but idly, without truth.

In the Bible a *name* is the intimate truth of things and, above all, of individuals. A name often represents a mission. For example, Abraham in Genesis (cf. 17:5) and Simon Peter in the Gospels (cf. *Jn* 1:42) received a new name to indicate the change in the direction of their lives. And truly knowing the name of God leads to the transformation of one's life: from the moment Moses learned God's name, his story changed (cf. *Ex* 3:13-15).

In Hebrew rites, the name of God was solemnly proclaimed on the Great Day of Forgiveness, when the people were forgiven because, through one's name, one comes into contact with God's very life, which is mercy.

Thus, "*to take the name of God upon oneself*" means to assume his reality, to enter into a strong relationship, a close relationship with him. For us Christians, this Commandment is the call to remind ourselves that we were baptised "*in the name of the Father and of the Son and of the Holy Spirit*", as we affirm each time we make the sign of the Cross, in order to carry out our daily actions in heartfelt and true communion with God, that is, in his love. And on this topic, making the sign of the Cross, I would like to repeat once again: teach your children to make the sign of the Cross. Have you seen how children do it? If you say to children: "make the sign of the Cross", they do something that they do not know about. They do not know how to make the sign of the Cross! Teach them how to do it: in the name of the Father, of the Son and of the Holy Spirit. A child's first act of faith. This is your homework, homework to do: teach children to make the sign of the Cross.

One may wonder: is it possible to take the name of God upon oneself in a hypocritical way, as an empty formality? Unfortunately, the answer is in the affirmative. Yes, it is possible. One can live in a false relationship with God. Jesus used to say of the doctors of the law: they did some things, but they did not do what God wanted. They spoke of God, but they did not do God's will. The advice that Jesus gives us is: "Do what they say but not what they do". One can have a false relationship with God, like those people. And this precept from the Decalogue is precisely an invitation to have a relationship with God that is not false, that is without hypocrisy; a relationship in which we entrust ourselves to him with all that we are. After all, until the day we stake everything on the Lord, by experiencing first-hand that life can be found in him, we are only theorising.

This is Christianity which moves hearts. Why are saints able to move hearts? Because not only do saints speak, they act! Our hearts are moved when a saint speaks to us, tells us things. And they are able to do so because, in saints, we can see what our heart profoundly desires: authenticity, true relationships, radicalism. And this can also be seen in "the saints next door" who, for example, are the many parents who set for their children an example of a consistent, simple, honest and generous life.

If more Christians were to take God's name upon themselves without falsehood – by honouring the first request of the Our Father: "*hallowed be thy name*" – the Church's message would receive more attention and would be more credible. If our daily life were to manifest God's name, we would see how beautiful Baptism is and what a great gift the Eucharist is; what sublime union there is between our body and the Body of Christ; Christ in us and we in him! United! This is not hypocrisy, this is truth. This is not speaking or praying like a parrot. This is praying from the heart, loving the Lord.

From the Cross of Christ onwards, no one can despise themselves and think badly of their life. No one and never! No matter what they may have done. Because *the name of each of us is on Christ's shoulders*. He carries us! It is worthwhile to take God's name upon ourselves because he took our names upon himself, to the very end, including the evil that is within us. He burdened himself, in order to forgive us, to place his love in our hearts. This is why in this Commandment, God proclaimed: "Take me upon yourself as I have taken you upon me."

Anyone, in whatever situation they may be, can invoke the Holy name of the Lord, who is faithful and merciful Love. God will never say "no" to a heart that invokes him sincerely. And let us return to the assignment to be done at home: teach children to make the sign of the Cross properly.

General Audience, 22nd August 2018, St Peter's Square

The Day of Rest

The journey through the Decalogue takes us to the Commandment regarding the day of rest. It sounds like an easy command to respect, but that is the wrong impression. True rest is not simple, because there is false rest and true rest. How can we recognise them?

Today's society thirsts for amusement and holidays. The entertainment industry is really flourishing, and advertising portrays the ideal world as one great amusement park where everyone has fun. The prevailing concept of *life* today does not have its centre of gravity in activity and commitment, but in *escapism*. Earning money to have fun, to satisfy oneself. The model is the image of a successful person who can afford ample room for diverse forms of enjoyment. But this mentality makes one slip toward the dissatisfaction of a life anaesthetised by fun that is not rest, but alienation and the escape from reality. Man has never rested as much as today, yet man has never experienced as much emptiness as today! Opportunities to amuse oneself, to go out, cruises, travels; but many things do not give you fulness of heart. Indeed: they do not give you rest.

The words of the Decalogue seek and find the crux of the problem, casting a different light on what rest is. The Commandment has a particular element: it provides a motive. Rest in the name of the Lord has a precise reason: "For in six days the Lord made heaven and earth, the sea, and all that is in them, and rested the seventh day; therefore the Lord blessed the Sabbath day and hallowed it" (*Ex* 20:11).

This takes us back to the end of creation, when God says: "God saw everything that he had made, and behold, it was very good" (*Gen* 1:31). And so begins the day of rest, which is God's joy for all that he has created. It is the day of contemplation and blessing.

What, then, is rest according to this commandment? It is the moment of contemplation, it is the moment of praise, not that of escapism. It is the time to look at reality and say: how beautiful life is! Contrary to rest as an escape from reality, the Decalogue proposes rest as the *blessing of reality*. For us Christians, the centre of the Lord's day, Sunday, is the Eucharist, which means "*thanksgiving*". It is the day to say to God: thank you Lord for life, for your mercy, for all your gifts. Sunday is not the day to forget the other days but to remember them, bless them and make peace with life. How many people there are who have many opportunities to amuse themselves, who are not at peace with life! Sunday is the day to make peace with life, saying: life is precious; it is not easy, sometimes it is painful, but it is precious.

To be introduced to authentic rest is a work of God in us, but it requires us to distance ourselves from the devil and his attraction (cf. Apostolic Exhortation *Evangelii Gaudium*, 83). In fact, it is very easy for the heart to succumb to unhappiness, dwelling on reasons for discontent. Blessing and joy imply an openness to good that is a mature movement of the heart. Goodness is loving and is never imposed. It is chosen.

Peace is chosen; it cannot be imposed and it is not found by chance. Distancing himself from the bitter wounds of his heart, man needs to make peace with what he is fleeing from. It is necessary to reconcile oneself with one's own history, with facts that one does not accept, with the difficult parts of one's own existence. I ask you: is each of you reconciled with your own history? A question to ponder: am I reconciled with my own history? True peace, in fact, is not about changing one's own history but about welcoming it and valuing it, just as it has unfolded.

How many times have we met sick Christians who have comforted us with a serenity that is not found in pleasure-seekers and hedonists! And we have seen humble and poor people rejoice in little graces with a happiness that knew of eternity.

The Lord says in Deuteronomy: "I have set before you life and death, blessing and curse; therefore choose life, that you and your descendants may live" (30:19). This choice is the "*fiat*" of the Virgin Mary; it is an opening to the Holy Spirit who places us in the footsteps of Christ, the One who gives himself to the Father in the most dramatic moment and thus takes the path that leads to the Resurrection.

When does life become beautiful? When we begin to think well of it, whatever our history. When the gift of a doubt makes its way: that all is grace,[21] and that holy thought breaks down the inner wall of dissatisfaction, giving way to authentic rest. Life becomes beautiful when the heart opens to providence and one discovers that what the Psalm says is true: "For God alone my soul waits in silence" (62[61]:2; 5). This passage from the Psalm is beautiful: "For God alone my soul waits in silence".

General Audience, 5th September 2018, St Peter's Square

---

[21] As St Thérèse of the Child Jesus reminds us in G. Bernanos' *Diary of a Country Priest*, Milan, 1965, 270.

The Day of Rest, Prophecy of Liberation

We return again to the *Third Commandment*, the one regarding the day of rest. The Decalogue proclaimed in the Book of Exodus is repeated in the Book of Deuteronomy almost identically, except for this Third Word in which a precious difference appears: whereas in Exodus the motive for rest is the *blessing of creation*, in Deuteronomy, it commemorates the *end of slavery*. On this day, the slave has to rest just like the owner, to celebrate the memory of the Passover of liberation.

Indeed, by definition, slaves cannot rest. But there are many forms of slavery, both interior and external constraints. There are exterior coercions such as oppression, lives seized by violence and other types of injustice. There are interior prisons which are, for example, mental blocks, complexes, character limitations and more. Is there rest under these conditions? Can a recluse or an oppressed man or woman be free? And can a person who is tormented by inner difficulties be free?

Actually, there are people who experience great freedom of spirit even in prison. Let us think for example of St Maximilian Kolbe or Cardinal Van Thuan who transformed dark oppression into places of light. There are also people marked by great interior fragility who, however, know about the rest of mercy and how to transmit this. God's mercy frees us. And when you encounter God's mercy, you feel great interior freedom and you are also able to transmit it. This is why it is important to open oneself to God's mercy so as not to be slaves to ourselves.

What then is true freedom? Does it consist, perhaps, in the freedom of choice? Certainly, this is part of freedom and we commit ourselves to ensure this to every man and woman (cf. Second Vatican Ecumenical Council, Pastoral Constitution *Gaudium et Spes*, 73). But we very well know that being able to do what one wants is not enough to be truly free, nor even to be happy. True freedom is much more.

Indeed, there is slavery which shackles more than a prison, more than a panic attack, more than any other kind of imposition: it is *slavery to one's ego*.[22] Those people who spend the whole day in front of the mirror in order to see their ego. And one's own ego is taller than one's body. They are slaves to their ego. One's ego can become a slave driver that tortures a person wherever he or she is, and causes that person the greatest oppression, namely "*sin*", which is not the banal breach of a code, but the failure of existence and the condition of slavery (cf. *Jn* 8:34).[23] In the end, the ego is sin, saying: "I want to do this and I do not care if there is a limit, if there is a commandment, and I do not even care if there is love".

Let us think, for example of ego in human passions: the glutton, the lustful, the miserly, the quick tempered, the envious, the bitter, the arrogant – and so forth –

---

[22] Cf. *Catechism of the Catholic Church*, n. 1733: "The choice to disobey and do evil is an abuse of freedom and leads to 'the slavery of sin'".

[23] Cf. *Catechism of the Catholic Church*, n. 1739: "Freedom and sin. Man's freedom is limited and fallible. In fact, man failed. He freely sinned. By refusing God's plan of love, he deceived himself and became a slave to sin. This first alienation engendered a multitude of others. From its outset, human history attests the wretchedness and oppression born of the human heart in consequence of the abuse of freedom".

they are slaves to their vices which oppress and torment them. There is no relief for the greedy because gluttony is the hypocrisy of the stomach that is full but makes one think it is empty. The hypocritical stomach makes one a glutton. We are slaves to the hypocritical stomach. There is no respite for the glutton and the lustful who must live for pleasure; the anxiety of possession destroys the miser; they always hoard money, hurting others; the fire of anger and the woodworm of envy ruin relationships. Writers say that envy makes the body and soul yellow, like a person with hepatitis: they turn yellow. The envious have a yellow soul because they can never have the fresh complexion of a healthy soul. Envy destroys. Bitterness which eschews all effort and makes life impossible; arrogant egocentricity; that ego I was talking about digs a trench between itself and others.

Dear brothers and sisters, who then is the real slave? Who is the one who knows no rest? Those who are not capable of love! And all these vices, these sins, this egoism distance us from love and they make us unable to love. We are our own slaves and we cannot love because love is always outgoing.

The Third Commandment which invites us to celebrate freedom with rest is, for us Christians, a prophecy of the Lord Jesus who breaks the interior slavery of sin, in order to make mankind capable of loving. True love is true freedom: it detaches us from possession, rebuilds relationships, knows how to welcome and value others, transforms all toil into a joyful gift and makes us capable of communion. Love makes people free even in prison, even if one is weak and limited.

This is the freedom that we receive from our Saviour, our Lord Jesus Christ.

General Audience, 12th September 2018, St Peter's Square

Honour your Father and your Mother

On the journey within the Ten Words, we come to the Commandment on the father and mother. It speaks of the honour owed to parents. What is this "*honour*"? The Hebrew term indicates glory, value, literally "importance", consistent with reality. It is not a question of external forms but of truth. To honour God, in the Scriptures, means recognising his reality, acknowledging his presence; this is also expressed with rites, but above all it means giving God his proper place in life. Thus, honouring our father and mother also means recognising their importance with practical actions, which express dedication, affection and care. But it is more than this.

The Fourth Word has a particular characteristic: it is the Commandment that contains a result. In fact, it says: "Honour your father and your mother, as the Lord your God commanded you; *that your days may be prolonged, and that it may go well with you, in the land which the Lord your God gives you*" (*Dt* 5:16). Honouring our parents leads to a long and happy life. The word "well" in the Decalogue appears only linked to the relationship with parents.

This thousands-of-years-old wisdom declares what human sciences have been able to establish for just a little more than a century: that the influence of childhood marks our entire life. It can often be easy to understand if someone has grown up in a healthy and balanced environment. But likewise, it is easy to understand if a person has experienced neglect or violence. Our childhood is a bit like indelible ink; it is evident in tastes, in ways of being, even if some try to hide the wounds of their own origins.

But the Fourth Commandment tells us even more. It does not speak of parents' goodness; it does not ask that fathers and mothers be perfect. It speaks about an act of the child, apart from the merits of the parents, and says something extraordinary and liberating: even if not all parents are good and not every childhood serene, all children can be happy, because achieving a full and happy life depends on the proper recognition of those who have brought us into the world.

Let us think about how this Word can be constructive for many young people who come from stories of pain and for all those who have suffered in their own youth. Many saints – and countless Christians – after a painful childhood, have lived a luminous life, because, thanks to Jesus Christ, they became reconciled with life. Let us consider that young man – blessed now and next month a saint – Sulprizio, who at nineteen years of age ended his life reconciled, despite much suffering, with many issues, because his heart was at peace and he never denied his parents. Let us think of St Camillus de Lellis, who from a disorderly childhood built a life of love and of service; of St Josephine Bakhita, who grew up in terrible slavery; or of Blessed Carlo Gnocchi, orphaned and poor; and of St John Paul II himself, marked by the loss of his mother at a tender age.

People, from whatever background they come, receive from this Commandment the direction that leads to Christ: indeed, manifest in him is the true Father, who invites us to *be "born anew" from above* (cf. *Jn* 3:3-8). The enigma of our lives is illuminated when we discover that God has always prepared for us a life as his children, where every act is a mission received from him.

Our wounds begin to be strengths when we discover by grace that the true enigma is no longer "*why*" but "*for whom?*"; for whom did this happen to me? In view of what result did God mould me throughout my history? Here everything is overturned; everything becomes precious; everything becomes constructive. How can my even sad and painful experience become, in the light of love, a source of salvation for others – for whom? So we can begin to honour our parents with the freedom of adult children and with merciful acceptance of their limitations.[24]

---

[24] Cf. St Augustine, *Sermon on Matthew*, 72, a, 4: "Thus Christ teaches you to reject your parents, and at the same time to love them. Thus, parents are loved systematically and with the spirit of faith when they are not preferred over God: 'one who loves' – these are the words of the Lord – 'his father and mother more than me is not worthy of me'. With these words he almost seems to admonish you not to love them; but instead, on the contrary, he is admonishing you to love them. In fact, he could have said: 'one who loves his father or mother is not worthy of me'. But he did not say this, so as not to speak against the law given by him, since it was he who, through his servant Moses, gave the law in which it is written: 'Honour your father and your mother'. He did not promulgate a contrary law but confirmed it; then, he taught you the order; he did not eliminate the duty of love owed to parents: one who loves his father and mother, but more than me. Therefore, one must love them, but not more than me: God is God, man is man. Love your parents, obey your parents, honour your parents; but if God calls you to a more important mission, in which affection for your parents could be an impediment, respect the order, do not suppress charity".

Honour parents: they gave us life! If you are distant from your parents, make an effort and return, go back to them; perhaps they are elderly... They gave you life. Then, there is a habit among us to say bad things, even to curse... Please, never, never ever insult other people's parents. Never! One should never insult a mother, never insult a father. Never! Never! Take this interior decision yourselves: from now on I will never insult anyone's mother or father. They gave life! They must never be insulted.

This wonderful life is offered to us, not imposed: reborn in Christ is a grace to be freely accepted (cf. *Jn* 1:11-13), and it is the treasure of our Baptism, in which, by the work of the Holy Spirit, we have only one Father, the one in heaven (cf. *Mt* 23:9; *1 Cor* 8:6; *Eph* 4:6). Thank you!

General Audience, 19th September 2018, St Peter's Square

Do Not Kill

This catechesis is dedicated to the Fifth Word: *you shall not kill*. The Fifth Commandment: *you shall not kill*. We are already in the second part of the Decalogue, the part which deals with relationships with our neighbour. And, with its concise and categorical formulation, this commandment rises up like a wall to defend the basic values of human relationships. And what is the basic value in human relationships? The value of life.[25] Thus, *you shall not kill*.

One could say that all the evil carried out in the world can be summed up in this: contempt for life. Life is assailed by war, by organisations that exploit people – we read in newspapers or see in newscasts many facts – by speculations on creation and by the throwaway culture and by every system that subjugates human existence to calculated opportunities, while a scandalous number of people live in a state unworthy of mankind. This is having contempt for life, that is, in some way, killing.

A contradictory approach even permits the termination of human life in the maternal womb, in the name of safeguarding other rights. But how can an action that ends

---

[25] Cf. Congregation for the Doctrine of the Faith, Instruction *Donum Vitae*, 5: AAS 80 (1988), 76-77: "Human life is sacred because from its beginning it involves 'the creative action of God' and it remains forever in a special relationship with the Creator, who is its sole end. God alone is the Lord of life from its beginning until its end: no one can, in any circumstance, claim for himself the right to destroy directly an innocent human being".

an innocent and defenceless life in its blossoming stage be therapeutic, civilised or simply human? I ask you: is it right to "do away with" a human life in order to solve a problem? Is it right to hire a hit man in order to solve a problem? One cannot. It is not right to "do away with" a human being, however small, in order to solve a problem. It is like hiring a hit man to solve a problem.

Where does all this come from? Violence and the rejection of life; where do they actually come from? From fear. Indeed, welcoming others is a challenge to individualism. Let us think, for example, about when it is discovered that a new life has a disability, even a serious one. In these tragic cases, parents need true closeness, true solidarity to face the reality and overcome the understandable fears. However, they often receive hasty advice to interrupt the pregnancy, which is an expression: "interrupting the pregnancy" means "doing away with someone", directly.

A sick child is like any other needy person on earth, like an elderly person who needs assistance, like many poor people who struggle to get by. He or she who is seen as a problem is in reality a gift from God that can save me from egocentrism and help me to grow in love. Vulnerable life shows us the way out, the way to save ourselves from a life that withdraws into itself and to discover the joy of love. And here I would like to pause to thank, to thank the many volunteers, to thank Italy's strong volunteerism, the strongest I have ever known. Thank you.

And what leads man to reject life? It is the idols of this world: money – better to get rid of this one because it will be costly; power, success. These are the wrong parameters for evaluating life. What is the only authentic measure of life? It is love, the love with which God loves it! The love with which God loves life: this is the measure. The love with which God loves all human life.

Indeed, what is the positive meaning of the Word "you shall not kill"? That God is a "*lover of life*", as we heard a short time ago in the Bible passage.

The secret of life is revealed to us by the way it was regarded by the Son of God who became man, to the point of assuming on the Cross rejection, weakness, poverty and suffering (cf. *Jn* 13:1). In every sick child, in every weak elderly person, in every desperate migrant, in every fragile and threatened life, Christ is seeking us (cf. *Mt* 25:34-46), he is seeking our heart, to open us up to the joy of love.

It is worthwhile to welcome every life because every man and woman is worth the blood of Christ himself (cf. *1 Pt* 1:18-19). We cannot have contempt for what God has loved so much!

We must tell the men and women of the world: do not have contempt for life! The life of others, but also one's own life because the Commandment "you shall not kill" applies to it too. Many young people should be told, "do not have contempt for your life. Stop rejecting God's work! You are a work of God! Do not underestimate yourself, do not despise yourself with the addictions that will ruin you and lead you to death!"

May no one measure life according to the deceptions of this world, but instead may each one accept him or herself and others in the name of the Father who created us. He is a "*lover of life*": this is beautiful. "God is a lover of life." And we are all so dear to him that he sent his Son for us. In fact, the Gospel says: "For God so loved the world that he gave his only Son; that whoever believes in him should not perish but have eternal life" (*Jn* 3:16).

General Audience, 10th October 2018, St Peter's Square

"Do Not Kill" according to Jesus

I would like to continue the catechesis on the Fifth Word of the Decalogue, "*You shall not kill*". We have already emphasised how this Commandment reveals that in God's eyes human life is precious, sacred and inviolable. No one can have contempt for his own or another's life; indeed, man bears God's image within and is the object of his infinite love, in whatever condition he was called into existence.

In the Gospel passage we listened to a short time ago, Jesus reveals to us an even deeper meaning of this Commandment. He affirms that, before God's tribunal, even ire against a brother or sister is a form of murder. This is why the Apostle John would write: "Anyone who hates his brother is a murderer" (*1 Jn* 3:15). But Jesus does not stop at this, and in the same logic he adds that even insult and contempt can kill. And we are used to insulting, it is true. We tend to insult like exhaling. And Jesus tells us: "Stop, because an insult does harm; it kills." Contempt. "But I detest these people, this person." And this is a way of killing a person's dignity. It would be nice if this teaching of Jesus were to enter the mind and heart, and each of us would say: "I will never insult anyone." It would be a fine objective, because Jesus tells us: "Look, if you harbour contempt, if you insult, if you hate, this is murder."

No human code equates such different acts, assigning them the same level of justice. And consistently, Jesus actually exhorts us to interrupt the offering of sacrifice in the Temple if we remember that we have offended a brother, in order to go and find him and reconcile with him. Also, when we go to Mass, we should have this attitude of reconciliation with the people we have had differences with. Even if we have thought ill of them, we have insulted them. But many times, while we are waiting for the priest to come and say Mass, we gossip a little and speak ill of others. But we cannot do this. Let us think about the gravity of an insult, of contempt, of hatred: Jesus equates them to killing.

What does Jesus mean by extending the field of the Fifth Word to this point? Man has a noble, very sensitive life, and has a hidden "I" no less important than his physical being. Indeed, an inopportune phrase is enough to offend the innocence of a child. A cold gesture can suffice to wound a woman. To break a young person's heart, it suffices to rebuff his confidence. To annihilate a man, it suffices to ignore him. Indifference kills. It is like telling the other person: "you are dead to me", because you have killed him in your heart. Not loving is the first step to killing; and *not killing* is the first step to loving.

At the beginning of the Bible, we read the terrible phrase that issues from the lips of the first murderer, Cain, after the Lord asks him where his brother is. Cain responds:

"I do not know; am I my brother's keeper?" (*Gen* 4:9)[26] This is how assassins speak: "it is not my concern", "that is your business", and similar assertions. Let us try to answer this question: are we our brothers' keepers? Yes, we are! We are each other's keepers! And this is the path to life; it is the path of not killing.

Human life needs love. And what is authentic love? It is what Christ showed us, namely, mercy. The love we cannot forego is forgiveness, which accepts those who have wronged us. None of us can survive without mercy; we all need forgiveness. Therefore, if to kill means to destroy, terminate, eliminate someone, then *not to kill* would mean to care for, appreciate, include. And also forgive.

No one can delude him or herself: "I am fine because I do nothing wrong." A mineral or plant has this type of existence, however, man does not. A person – man or woman – does not. More is asked of a man or woman. There is good to be done, prepared for each of us, each his or her own, which makes us ourselves at the core. "*You shall not kill*" is an appeal to love and mercy; it is a call to live according to the Lord Jesus, who gave his life for us and rose for us. Once, here in the Square, we all repeated together a saint's expression about this. Perhaps it will help

---

[26] Cf. *Catechism of the Catholic Church*, n. 2259: "In the account of Abel's murder by his brother Cain, Scripture reveals the presence of anger and envy in man, consequences of original sin, from the beginning of human history. Man has become the enemy of his fellow man. God declares the wickedness of this fratricide: 'What have you done? The voice of your brother's blood is crying to me from the ground. And now you are cursed from the ground, which has opened its mouth to receive your brother's blood from your hand' (*Gen* 4:10-11)".

us: "It is good to do no wrong, but it is wrong to do no good." We must always do good; go a step further.

The Lord, who by becoming flesh sanctified our existence; he, who with his blood made our life invaluable; he, "the Author of life" (*Acts* 3:15), thanks to whom each one is a gift of the Father. In him, in his love stronger than death, and by the power of the Spirit whom the Father gives us, we can accept the Word "*You shall not kill*" as the most important and essential appeal: that is, "you shall not kill" signifies a call to love.

General Audience, 17th October 2018, St Peter's Square

Do Not Commit Adultery

Our series of catecheses on the Commandments brings us today to the Sixth Word, which addresses the emotional and sexual dimension, and states: "*You shall not commit adultery*".

The immediate call is to fidelity, and indeed no human relationship is authentic without fidelity and loyalty.

One cannot love only as long as it is "convenient"; love is truly manifested beyond the threshold of one's own personal advantage, when one gives unreservedly. As the *Catechism* states: "Love seeks to be definitive; it cannot be an arrangement 'until further notice'" (n. 1646). Fidelity is an attribute of a free, mature and responsible human relationship. Friends, too, reveal themselves as authentic because they remain so in all circumstances, otherwise they are not friends. Christ reveals authentic love; the One who lives in the boundless love of the Father is, on this strength, the faithful Friend who welcomes us even when we err, and who always wants good for us, even when we do not deserve it.

Human beings need to be loved unconditionally and those who do not receive this acceptance carry a certain incompleteness within themselves, often without knowing it. The human heart seeks to fill this void with surrogates, accepting compromises and mediocrity that have only a vague flavour of love. The risk is to call certain bitter and immature relationships "love", with the illusion of finding the light of life in something that, at best, is merely a reflection of it.

Thus it can happen, for example, that one overestimates physical attraction, which is itself a gift from God, but aims to pave the way for an authentic and faithful relationship with the person. As St John Paul II used to say, the human being "is called to a full and mature spontaneity of relationships", which is "the gradual fruit of discerning the impulses in one's own heart". It is something that is acquired, because every human being must "learn with determination and consistency what the body signifies" (cf. Catechesis, 12th November 1980).

The call to married life, therefore, requires a heartfelt discernment of the quality of the relationship and a period of engagement to confirm it. To approach the Sacrament of Marriage, the engaged couple must establish the certainty that the hand of God is in their bond and that he precedes and accompanies them and will enable them to say: *With the Grace of Christ I promise to be faithful to you always.* They cannot promise each other fidelity "*in good times and in bad, in sickness and in health*", and to love and honour one another all the days of their lives, solely on the basis of good will or of the hope that it "will work out". They need to ground themselves on the solid terrain of God's faithful love. And this is why, before receiving the Sacrament of Matrimony, there should be a careful preparation, I would say a catechumenate, because with love one's entire life is at stake, and one does not kid around with love. Three or four meetings in the parish church cannot be defined as "marriage preparation": no, this is not preparation: this is feigned preparation. And the responsibility falls on those who do this: on the parish priest, on the bishop who permits these things.

The preparation must be mature and it takes time. It is not a formality: it is a Sacrament. But it must be prepared with a true catechumenate.

Indeed, fidelity is a way of being, a style of life. One works with loyalty, one speaks with sincerity, one remains faithful to the truth in one's thoughts, in one's actions. A life woven of fidelity is expressed in all dimensions and leads to being faithful and reliable men and women in every circumstance.

However, to achieve such a beautiful life, our human nature is not enough. God's fidelity needs to enter our being, to infect us. This Sixth Word calls us to turn our gaze to Christ whose fidelity can remove from us an adulterous heart and give us a faithful heart. In him and only in him, is there love without reservations and second thoughts, absolute and unmitigated giving, and the tenacity of full acceptance.

From his death and Resurrection comes our fidelity, from his unconditional love comes steadfastness in relationships. From communion with him, with the Father and with the Holy Spirit comes communion among us and the ability to live our bonds in fidelity.

General Audience, 24th October 2018, St Peter's Square

Our Spousal Vocation Finds Fulness in Christ

I would like to complete the catechesis on the Sixth Word of the Decalogue, "You shall not commit adultery", highlighting that the faithful love of Christ is the light by which to live the beauty of human affection. Indeed, our emotional dimension is a *call to love* that is manifested in fidelity, in welcoming, and in mercy. This is very important. How is love manifested? In fidelity, in welcoming, and in mercy.

It must not be forgotten however, that this Commandment refers explicitly to marital fidelity and therefore it is fitting that we reflect more deeply on its *spousal* significance. This Scripture passage, this passage from the Letter of St Paul is revolutionary! Considering the anthropology of that age, it is saying that a husband must love his wife as Christ loves the Church: it is a revolution! Perhaps in those times it was the most revolutionary thing that had been said about marriage. Always on the path of love. We can ask: to whom is this command of fidelity addressed? Only to spouses? In reality, this command is for everyone; it is a paternal Word of God addressed to every man and woman.

Let us remember that the journey of human maturation is the same path of love that goes from *receiving care* to being able to *offer care*, from *receiving life* to being able to *give life*. Becoming adult men and women means developing the *spousal* and *parental* aptitude which is expressed in life's various situations, such as the ability to take someone else's burden upon oneself, and to love him or her unambiguously. It is therefore the overall ability of a person who accepts reality and is ready to enter into a profound relationship with others.

Who then is the adulterer, the lustful, the unfaithful? It is an immature person who keeps his life to himself and interprets situations on the basis of his own wellbeing and his own gratification. Therefore, in order *to get married*, the wedding ceremony does not suffice! We must make the journey from *I* to *we*, from thinking alone to thinking together, from living alone to living together: it is a good journey; it is a beautiful journey. Once we succeed at decentralising ourselves, all action is *spousal*: we work, we speak, we decide, we meet others with a welcoming and oblational attitude.

In this sense every Christian vocation – we can now expand the perspective further and say that in this sense every Christian vocation – is *spousal*. The *priesthood* is such because it is a call in Christ and in the Church, to serve the community with all the affection, the tangible care and the wisdom that the Lord gives us. The Church does not need people who aspire to the role of priests – no, we do not need them, it is better if they stay home; rather, we need men whose hearts are touched by the Holy Spirit with an unreserved love for the Bride of Christ. The priestly ministry means loving the People of God with all the paternal care, the tenderness and strength of a spouse and a father. Thus *virginity* consecrated in Christ is also lived with fidelity and with joy as a spousal and fruitful relationship of motherhood and fatherhood.

I repeat: every Christian vocation is spousal because it is the fruit of the bond of love in which we are all regenerated, a bond of love with Christ, as we were reminded by the passage from Paul that was read at the beginning. Starting from *his* fidelity, from *his* tenderness, from *his* generosity, we look to marriage and every vocation with faith, and we understand the full meaning of sexuality.

The human creature in his or her inseparable unity to the Spirit and to the body, and in the male and female polarity, is a very good reality which is destined to love and to be loved. The human body is not an instrument of pleasure, but the setting for our call to love, and there is no room for lust or superficiality in authentic love. Men and women deserve more than this!

Thus the Word, "You shall not commit adultery", despite its negative form, directs us to our original call, that is, to the full and faithful spousal love which Jesus Christ revealed and gave to us (cf. *Rom* 12:1).

General Audience, 31st October 2018, St Peter's Square

Do Not Steal

Continuing the explanation of the Decalogue, we come to the Seventh Word: *"You shall not steal"*.

In hearing this Commandment we think of the theme of theft and of respect for other people's property. There is no culture in which theft and the abuse of property are legal; human sensibility, in fact, is very sensitive in regard to the defence of property.

But it is worth opening ourselves up to a broader interpretation of this Word, focusing on the theme of the ownership of goods in the light of Christian wisdom.

The Social Doctrine of the Church speaks of the *universal destination of goods*. What does it mean? Let us listen to what the *Catechism* says: "In the beginning God entrusted the earth and its resources to the common stewardship of mankind to take care of them, master them by labour, and enjoy their fruits. The goods of creation are destined for the whole human race" (n. 2402). Moreover: "The universal destination of goods remains primordial, even if the promotion of the common good requires respect for the right to private property and its exercise" (n. 2403).[27]

[27] Cf. Encyclical *Laudato Si'*, n. 67: "Each community can take from the bounty of the earth whatever it needs for subsistence, but it also has the duty to protect the earth and to ensure its fruitfulness for coming generations. 'The earth is the Lord's' (*Ps* 24:1); to him belongs 'the earth with all that is within it' (*Dt* 10:14). Thus God rejects every claim to absolute ownership: 'The land shall not be sold in perpetuity, for the land is mine; for you are strangers and sojourners with me' (*Lev* 25:23)".

Providence, however, did not create a world of identical objects; there are differences, different conditions, different cultures, so one can live by providing for one another. The world is rich in resources to ensure the basic necessities for everyone. Yet many live in scandalous indigence and resources, used indiscriminately, are dwindling. But there is only one world! There is only one humanity![28] Today the world's wealth is in the hands of the minority, of the few, and poverty, or rather misery and suffering, is in those of the many, of the majority.

If there is hunger on earth it is not for lack of food! Rather, due to market demands it is at times even destroyed, wasted. What is lacking is free and forward-looking entrepreneurship, which ensures proper production in a framework of solidarity, which ensures equitable distribution. The *Catechism* also states: "In his use of things man should regard the external goods he legitimately owns not merely as exclusive to himself but common to others also, in the sense that they can benefit others as well as himself" (n. 2404). All wealth, in order to be good, must have a social dimension.

The positive and broad meaning of the commandment "*you shall not steal*" appears in this perspective. "The

---

[28] Cf. Paul VI, Encyclical *Populorum Progressio*, n. 17: "Each man is also a member of society; hence he belongs to the community of man. It is not just certain individuals but all men who are called to further the development of human society as a whole... We are the heirs of earlier generations, and we reap benefits from the efforts of our contemporaries; we are under obligation to all men. Therefore we cannot disregard the welfare of those who will come after us to increase the human family. The reality of human solidarity brings us not only benefits but also obligations".

ownership of any property makes its holder a steward of providence" (*ibid.*). No one is the absolute owner of goods: he is a steward of goods. Ownership is a *responsibility*: "But I am rich in everything..." – this is a responsibility that you have. And every good subtracted from the logic of God's providence is betrayed; it is betrayed in its most profound sense. What I truly own is what I am able to give. This is the measure to evaluate how I am able to manage riches, whether good or bad; this phrase is important: what I truly own is what I am able to give. If I am able to give, I am open, then I am rich not only in what I own, but also in generosity, generosity also as a duty to give wealth, so that all may partake of it. In fact, if I cannot give something it is because that thing owns me, has power over me, and enslaves me. The possession of goods is an opportunity to multiply them creatively and to use them generously, and thereby to grow in charity and freedom.

Christ himself, "though he was in the form of God, did not count equality with God a thing to be grasped, but emptied himself" (*Phil* 2:6-7) and enriched us with his poverty (cf. *2 Cor* 8:9).

While humanity takes pains *to have more*, God redeems it by becoming poor: that Crucified Man paid an incalculable ransom for everyone, on the part of God the Father, "rich in mercy" (*Eph* 2:4; cf. *Jas* 5:11). What makes us rich is not goods but love. So often we have heard what the People of God say: "The devil enters through the pockets." It starts with a love of money, a hunger for possessions; then comes vanity: "Ah, I am rich and brag about it"; and, in the end, pride and arrogance. This is the devil's way of acting in us. But the entrance is through the pocket.

Dear brothers and sisters, once again Jesus Christ reveals to us the full meaning of Scripture. *"You shall not steal"* means: love with your goods, make use of your means to love as best you can. Then your life becomes good and your property truly becomes a gift. Because life is not the time for possessing but for loving. Thank you.

General Audience, 7th November 2018, St Peter's Square

Don't Bear False Witness

In this catechesis we will address the Eighth Word of the Decalogue: *"You shall not bear false witness against your neighbour"*.

This Commandment – the *Catechism* says – "forbids misrepresenting the truth in our relations with others" (n. 2464). To live with false communication is serious because it impedes relationships and, therefore, impedes love. Where there are lies there is no love; there can be no love. And when we speak about interpersonal communication we do not mean words alone, but also gestures, attitudes, even silence and absence. A person *speaks* with all that he is and does. We are always communicating. We all live by communicating and we are always poised between truth and lies.

But what does it mean to *tell the truth*? Does it mean being sincere? Or precise? In fact, this is not enough, because one can be genuinely mistaken, or one can be precise in the details but not grasp the overall sense. At times we justify ourselves by saying: "But I said what I felt!" Yes, but you have presented your point of view as an absolute. Or: "I only told the truth!" Perhaps, but you revealed personal or private matters. How much gossip destroys communion by inopportune comments or lack of sensitivity! Indeed, gossip kills, and James the Apostle said this in his Letter. Those who gossip are people who kill: they kill others because the tongue kills as much as a knife. Be careful! Those who gossip are like terrorists because their tongues throw a bomb and then they calmly walk away, but what they say with that bomb destroys the reputation of others. Do not forget: gossiping kills.

So: what is truth? This is the question Pilate asked, just as Jesus, standing before him, fulfilled the Eighth Commandment (cf. *Jn* 18:38). Indeed, the words "you shall not bear false witness against your neighbour" pertain to forensic language. The Gospels culminate in the narrative of Jesus's Passion, Death and Resurrection; and this is the narrative of a process, of the execution of the sentence and of an unprecedented consequence.

As he is interrogated by Pilate, Jesus says: "For this I was born, and for this I have come into the world, *to bear witness to the truth*" (*Jn* 18:37). And Jesus bears this "witness" through his Passion and through his death. The Evangelist Mark recounts that "the centurion, who stood facing him, saw that he thus breathed his last, [and] said: 'Truly this man was the Son of God!'" (15:39). Yes, because he was consistent. He was consistent: in the way that he dies, Jesus manifests the Father, his merciful and steadfast love.

Truth is fully realised in the very person of Jesus (cf. *Jn* 14:6), in his *way* of living and of dying, fruit of his relationship with the Father. This existence as children of God. He, the Risen One, gives it to us too, sending the Holy Spirit who is the Spirit of truth, who attests to our heart that God is our Father (cf. *Rom* 8:16).

In every action, man, people, either affirm or deny this truth. From the little everyday situations to the most binding choices. But the logic is always the same: what our parents and grandparents teach us when they tell us not to tell lies.

Let us ask ourselves: to what truths do our – we Christians' – deeds, our words, our choices, attest? Everyone can ask themselves: am I a witness of truth, or am I more or less a liar disguised as *true*? Everyone ask themselves. We Christians are not exceptional men and women. However, we are children of the heavenly Father, who is good and does not disappoint us, and instils in our hearts love for our brothers and sisters. This truth is not expressed so much in speech; it is a way of life, a way of living, and is seen in every single action (cf. *Jas* 2:18). This man is a *true* man, that woman is a *true* woman: one can see it. But how, if they do not open their mouths? But they behave like *true* men and women. They tell the truth, they act with truth. It is a good way for us to live.

The truth is the marvellous revelation of God, of his Fatherly face; it is his boundless love. This truth corresponds to human reason, but infinitely transcends it, because it is a gift descended to the earth and embodied in Christ crucified and risen; it is made visible by those who belong to him and demonstrate his same disposition.

Not bearing false witness means living as children of God, who never, ever contradict themselves, never tell lies; living as children of God, letting shine forth in every deed the supreme truth: that God is Father and that we can trust in him. I trust God: this is the great truth. From our trust in God – who is Father and who loves me, loves us – springs my truth, being truthful and not a liar.

General Audience, 14th November 2018, St Peter's Square

Do Not Covet your Neighbour's Wife; Do Not Covet your Neighbour's Goods

Our sessions on the Decalogue lead us to the last Commandment. We heard it at the opening. These are not only the final words of the text, but much more: they are the fulfilment of the journey through the Decalogue, touching the heart of all that it consigns. In fact, on a closer look, no new content is being added: the indications "*you shall not covet your neighbour's wife*" and "*you shall not covet your neighbour's goods*" are at least latent in the Commandments on adultery and theft; so what is the function of these words? Is it a summary? Is it something more?

Let us keep well in mind that the purpose of all the Commandments is to indicate life's boundaries, the limits beyond which man destroys himself and neighbour, ruining his relationship with God. If you go beyond these, you destroy yourself, you also destroy your relationship with God and your relationship with others. The Commandments point this out. Through this last word the fact is emphasised that all transgressions spring from a common inner root: *evil desires*. All sins are born from an evil desire. All. There, the heart begins to move and one sets out on that wave and ends up in transgression. But not a formal, legal transgression: a transgression that wounds oneself and others.

In the Gospel Jesus says it explicitly: "from within, out of the heart of man, come evil thoughts, fornication, theft, murder, adultery, coveting, wickedness, deceit, licentiousness, envy, slander, pride, foolishness. All these evil things come from within, and they defile a man" (*Mk* 7:21-23).

Thus we understand that the whole itinerary outlined by the Decalogue would have no utility whatsoever if it did not reach this level, *the heart of man*. Where do these awful things come from? The Decalogue is clear and profound in this aspect: this journey's point of arrival – the last Commandment – is the heart, and if this, if the heart is not liberated, the rest serves little purpose. This is the challenge: to liberate the heart from all these evil and awful things. God's precepts can be reduced to being no more than the lovely facade of a life that nevertheless continues to be an existence of slaves, not of children. Often, something unsightly and unresolved is hidden behind the pharisaic mask of suffocating propriety.

We must instead allow ourselves to be unmasked by these Commandments on desire, so they may show us our poverty, in order to lead us to a holy humiliation. Each of us can ask ourselves: which awful desires do I most often feel? Envy, greed, gossip? All these things that come to me from inside. We each can ask ourselves this and it will do us good. Man needs this blessed humiliation: by which he discovers he cannot free himself on his own, which is why he cries out to God in order to be saved. Paul explains it in an unparalleled way, referring precisely to the Commandment *you shall not covet* (*Rom* 7:7-24).

It is vain to think we can correct ourselves without the gift of the Holy Spirit. It is vain to think we can purify our heart through a tremendous effort of our own will: this is not possible. We must open ourselves to the relationship with God, in truth and in freedom: only in this way can our efforts bear fruit, because the Holy Spirit is there to carry us forward.

The task of Biblical Law is not to delude man that literal obedience leads him to a contrived but unreachable salvation. The Law's task is to lead man to his truth, or to his poverty, which becomes the authentic opening and personal opening to God's mercy, which transforms us and renews us. God is the only one able to renew our heart, provided we open our heart to him: it is the sole condition. He does everything but we must open our heart to him.

The final words of the Decalogue teach everyone to acknowledge that we are *beggars*; they help us to face the turmoil of our heart, in order to stop living selfishly and to become poor in spirit, authentic in the sight of God, allowing ourselves to be redeemed by the Son and to be tempered by the Holy Spirit. The Holy Spirit is the teacher who guides us: let us allow ourselves to be helped. We are beggars, let us ask for this grace.

"Blessed are the poor in spirit, for theirs is the kingdom of heaven" (*Mt* 5:3). Yes, blessed are those who stop deluding themselves into believing that they can save themselves from their own weaknesses without God's mercy which alone can heal. Only God's mercy can heal hearts. Blessed are those who recognise their evil desires and who, with a contrite and humbled heart, stand before God and others not as righteous but as sinners. What Peter said to the Lord is beautiful: "Depart from me, Lord, for I am a sinful man". This is a beautiful prayer: "Depart from me, Lord, for I am a sinful man".

They are the ones who know how to have compassion, who know how to have mercy for others because they experience it themselves.

General Audience, 21st November 2018, St Peter's Square

The New Law in Christ and Desires according to the Spirit

This catechesis, which concludes the series on the Ten Commandments, we can take as the key theme that of *desires*, which allows us to review the journey we have made and summarise the stages we have completed in reading the text of the Decalogue, always in the light of the full revelation in Christ.

We began with *gratitude* as the basis of the relationship of trust and obedience: God, as we saw, asked for nothing before he had given much more. He invites us to obedience in order to deliver us from the misleading forms of idolatry that have so much power over us. Indeed, seeking self-realisation in the idols of this world empties us and enslaves us, while what gives us stature and consistency is the relationship with the One who, in Christ, makes us children by virtue of his fatherhood (cf. *Eph* 3:14-16).

This entails a process of blessing and liberation, which is true, authentic rest. As the Psalm states: "For God alone my soul waits in silence; from him comes my salvation" (*Ps* 62[61]:1).

This liberated life embraces our personal history and reconciles us with what, from childhood to the present, we have experienced, becoming adults and being able to give the proper weight to the realities and the people in our life. By this path we enter a relationship with our neighbour which, springing from the love that God demonstrates in Jesus Christ, is a call to the beauty of *fidelity, generosity* and *authenticity*.

But to live in this way – that is, in the beauty of fidelity, generosity and authenticity – we need *a new heart*, inhabited by the Holy Spirit (cf. *Ez* 11:19; 36:26). I wonder: how does this heart "transplant", from an old heart to a new heart, come about? Through the gift of new desires (cf. *Rom* 8:6) that are sown in us by the grace of God, in a particular way, through the Ten Commandments fulfilled by Jesus, as he teaches in the Sermon on the Mount (cf. *Mt* 5:15-48). Indeed, in contemplating the life described in the Decalogue – that is, a grateful, free, authentic, blessed, adult existence, as guardian and lover of a steadfast, generous and sincere life – almost without realising it we stand before Christ again. The Decalogue is his "x-ray": it is like a photographic negative that lets his face appear – as in the Holy Shroud. And thus the Holy Spirit renders our heart fruitful, placing in it desires that are his gift, the *desires of the Spirit*. To desire according to the Spirit, to desire with the rhythm of the Spirit, to desire with the music of the Spirit.

Looking to Christ we see beauty, goodness, truth. And the Spirit engenders a life that, supporting these desires of his, kindles hope, faith and love in us.

In this way we can better understand why the Lord Jesus did not come to abolish the Law but to fulfil it, to develop it, and as the law according to the flesh was a series of prescriptions and prohibitions, according to the Spirit this same law becomes life (cf. *Jn* 6:63; *Eph* 2:15), because it is no longer a rule but the very flesh of Christ, who loves us, seeks us, forgives us, consoles us and in his Body recreates the communion with the Father, lost through the disobedience of sin. And thus, the literal negative, the negative expression used in the Commandments – "you shall not steal", "you shall not insult", "you shall not kill" – that "not" is transformed into a positive approach: to love, to make room in my heart for others, all desires that sow positivity. And this is the fulness of the law that Jesus came to bring us.

In Christ, and in him alone, the Decalogue ceases to be a condemnation (cf. *Rom* 8:1) and becomes the authentic truth of human life, namely, a desire for love – a desire for good, to do good is born here – a desire for joy, for peace, for magnanimity, for benevolence, for goodness, for fidelity, for meekness, self-control. It goes from that "no" to this "yes": the positive attitude of a heart that opens with the power of the Holy Spirit.

This is what seeking Christ in the Decalogue means: to make our heart fruitful so that it may be filled with love and open to God's work. When men and women comply with the desire to live according to Christ, they are opening the door to salvation which cannot fail to occur because God the Father is generous and, as the *Catechism* says, "thirsts that we may thirst for him" (n. 2560).

If evil desires defile mankind (cf. *Mt* 15:18-20), the Spirit places in our heart his holy desires which are the seeds of new life (cf. *1 Jn* 3:9). Indeed, the new life is not a titanic effort to comply with a rule, but rather, the new life is God's own Spirit that begins to guide us to his fruits, in a happy synergy between our joy in being loved and his joy in loving us. The two joys come together: God's joy in loving us and our joy in being loved.

This is what the Decalogue is for us Christians: to contemplate Christ in order to open ourselves up to receive his heart, to receive his will, to receive his Holy Spirit.

General Audience, 28th November 2018, St Peter's Square

THEMATIC INDEX